The Choose Yourself Guide to Wealth

Copyright © James Altucher

ALL RIGHTS RESERVED

No part of this publication may be reproduced, stored in or introduced into a retrieval system, or transmitted, in any form or by any means (electronically, mechanical, photocopying, recording or otherwise), without the prior written permission of both the copyright owner and the publisher of this book.

Re-selling through electronic outlets (like Amazon, Barnes and Nobles or E-bay) without permission of the publisher is illegal and punishable by law.

The scanning, uploading, and distribution of this book via the Internet or via any other means without the permission of the publisher is illegal and punishable by law.

Please purchase only authorized editions and no not participate in or encourage electronic piracy of copyrightable materials.

Your support of the author's right is appreciated.

ISBN-13: 978-1501009945 | ISBN-10:150100994x

COVER DESIGN AND LAYOUT: ERIN TYLER

CHOOSE YOURSELF
MEDIA LLC.

THE
CHOOSE
YOURSELF
GUIDE TO
WEALTH
★ ★ ★ ★ ★ ★

— JAMES —
ALTUCHER

WHAT PEOPLE ARE SAYING ABOUT JAMES ALTUCHER:

"This book is bold, empowering, and useful. It gave me the courage to turn down distractions so that I could focus on the important things in life, like endorsing this book. I would never say no to James partly because he is my cousin (genetically proven!)"

~A.J. JACOBS, 3 times New York Times best-selling author of 'My Life As An Experiment' and the pioneer behind the world's largest family reunion.

"Your freedom may be closer than you think. . . . I'm so grateful for this book and I know you will be, too."

~KRIS CARR, New York Times best-selling author of 'Crazy Sexy Diet'

"You can make a lot of money, no matter what your age. You can reinvent your retirement. You can become a successful writer, photographer, or consultant. You can get paid to travel the world or learn a new hobby. The list is endless. "

~PORTER STANSBERRY, founder of Stansberry & Associates Investment Research

"James Altucher is scary smart."

~STEPHEN J. DUBNER, 3 Times New York Times best-selling co-author of 'Freakonomics'

"I wish James had written this book fifty years ago."

~LOUISE HAY, Founder of Hay House, and New York Times best-selling author of 'You Can Heal Your Life', (over 100,000,000 copies sold).

WHAT PEOPLE ARE SAYING ABOUT *CHOOSE YOURSELF!*:

"James has become my go-to guy for getting my mind in the right place and my future on the right track. At fifty I feel like thirty and once again excited about what can be! Anyone interested in a new beginning and every young adult just starting out should read this book."

—BRIAN DICUS

"James Altucher has an irreverent way of looking at life, success, and happiness. He has a lot of insight on how the world is changing."

—HELLEN K. CLEVELAND

"Be forewarned. Reading this book is like choosing between the red pill and the blue pill in The Matrix. If you prefer the safety of the your own bed and believing what you want to believe then take the blue pill and don't read this book. However, if you want to see how deep the rabbit hole goes then take the red pill and read this book."

—DONALD MURRAY

"James is one of the most authentic voices out there. Read his books, follow his blog, and listen to his podcasts."

—ALAN BARNES

"The world has changed and we need to catch up. Since reading Altucher's blog about quitting your job in 2014, I've become an absolute Altucher addict. I suggest this and everything else you can get from him, podcasts, blogs."

—CHRISTOPHER KOSSOW

"This book got me and my partner motivated to start our own business."

—ERIC VON WELBAUM

"It's not about selfishness; it's about self worth. In other words, no one is more valuable or less valuable than me."

—CHRISTINE L WHEELER

"The two days I read this book in the a.m., before work, were two of my most productive days ever. Though I've finished it, I'm going to start the book over and make it required pre-work reading!"

—JENNIFER SILVERBERG

"James is very honest about his life. Both his Successes as well as his Failures. He is a relentless idea machine and forward thinker."

—DON M.

"I'm in the first year of my business and this book reminds me why I chose myself and why I will continue to blaze my own path."

—MARY HUANG

"This is one of the most honest analysis of work, business, and the psychology of being an individual and an entrepreneur. Changed my life and continues to daily."

—ANDY KING

"No holds barred, painfully honest, and joyfully blunt expose on why the most important choice you will ever make is you. Altucher has written a primer for life that should be required reading for every graduating high school senior. It may just save them from a life of mediocrity and despair."

—RAY HOLLISTER

I call *Choose Yourself!* a gift to all willing to receive it. I encourage everyone to accept it and start doing what James suggests. You'll bless not only yourself but also everyone in your growing circle of influence."

—KAREN HANSEN

"This book, and other materials by the author, helped me change my life. The Daily Practice is working for me."

—KRISTIN M.

"This isn't like any other book, and James is fortunately not like anyone else. The content is real, engaging and definitely life-changing"

—G. SANCHEZ

"Altucher is somewhere between Bukowski and Woody Allen. His self-hating personality is benign for all. Finally, a self-help book that does not pretend to help you. Judo with Altucher, and learn to fight yourself."

—ROBERT LOEBER

"The most honest and heart-wrenching book I have ever read. I feel as if my thinking has been reprogrammed and I actually started to smile once again."

—BRIAN MILLER

"Good read, good advice. Honest and openhearted work. I recommend this book to anyone looking to get "unstuck" Thanks, James."

—ONI R. WOODS

"If, like me, you are in the midst of a major life decision, I thoroughly recommend taking the time to read this to gain confidence in yourself and just live your life. I have only just finished this but I plan to read it again immediately. *Choose Yourself!* is totally worth its minimal price."

—NAKIAN

RECENT TESTIMONIALS:

"James, you inspired me to get off my butt. I've started to write down ten ideas a day to help my creativity and now demand my kids do the same. I've started the Daily Practice and already feel like a happier person. I don't know how to thank you enough. I'm a fan for life."

—NIK SEETHARAMAN

"I bought your book and was deeply influenced by your insights at a point in my life where I needed change. Since then I have quit my job, started a company and we are actually raising money. So just saying thanks, what you are doing matters."

—DAN DAREL

"It's Juan again. I was the guy who was making $25 writing a real estate blog. You guys were awesome enough to answer my question on how to make more money writing, back in episode 55 of Ask Altucher. Thank you so much! I've listened to the episode over 30 times. I wanted to give you a quick update on what's happened to me since then. I have indeed, started making more money. I now make $45 per blog post flat rate, plus a bonus if they reach over 1,000 views."

—JUAN GARGIULO

DEDICATION

When I dedicated *Choose Yourself!*, I couldn't think of a more fitting dedication than to myself. Not in a self-glorifying way but more in a way that would remind me each day that I needed to choose myself—to follow my own Daily Practice that I recommend.

Because a practice is just that—practice. It's not a solution. It's not a cure. It's something that has to be undertaken every day (or as much as possible) in order to work.

With this book I can safely get back to the norms of what dedication pages are all about.

THIS BOOK IS DEDICATED TO MY WIFE,
CLAUDIA AZULA ALTUCHER.

For being everything that I'm not.
For putting up with everything I am.
For stitching me together whenever I bleed.
For letting me surprise her.
For laughing whenever I joke with her.

Contents

INTRODUCTION: IDEAS ARE THE CURRENCY OF THE TWENTY-FIRST CENTURY.........................16

THE 18 NEW RULES OF ABUNDANCE.........................26

HOW I ENDED UP IN PRISON—AND HOW I BROKE OUT... 28

THE FACTS 32

THE HISTORY OF THE END OF THE WORLD 34

WHY ALL THE PERSONAL FINANCE GURUS ARE OUT OF DATE 40

DEVELOP A PRACTICE FOR SUCCESS 44

RESULTS OF THE DAILY PRACTICE 47

PART 1

NEW GAME, NEW RULES 49

WHAT IF YOU DON'T KNOW WHAT YOUR PASSION IS? 50

WHY YOU *HAVE* TO QUIT YOUR JOB THIS YEAR 52

BE AN IDEA MACHINE 60

HOW TO SELL ANYTHING 76

HOW TO CONVINCE ANYONE OF ANYTHING IN SIXTY SECONDS.........................84

ONCE THE IDEAS GET ROLLING . . . : TEN THINGS YOU NEED TO KNOW ABOUT LEADING.........................90

SHARING IDEAS: BEING A GREAT PUBLIC SPEAKER 98

DISCUSSING IDEAS: HOW TO NEGOTIATE WITH ANYONE 102

USING IDEAS TO CONNECT PEOPLE: BUILDING A PERMISSION NETWORK . 114

DEVELOPING HABITS FOR ABUNDANCE 120

HOW TO MASTER ANYTHING.. 120

GETTING RID OF YOUR EXCUSES..................................... 130

WHY TO-DO LISTS DON'T WORK...................................... 138

HAVE THEMES INSTEAD OF GOALS 139

PART 2

MAKING MONEY IN THE TWENTY-FIRST CENTURY 147

TRENDS: THE POWER TO SEE THINGS DIFFERENTLY THAN EVERYONE ELSE. 146

TREND #1 BIOTECH.. 150

TREND #2: HEALTHCARE.. 152

TREND #3 : OBSERVATION.. 153

TREND #4: THE TEMP WORKFORCE 154

TREND #5: ROBOTICS 155

TREND #6: CHEMISTRY... 156

TREND #7: FINANCIAL TECHNOLOGY 157

LESSONS I LEARNED FROM BUILDING A BUSINESS...................... 162

A CHEAT SHEET FOR STARTING A BUSINESS............................ 170

WHY I WANT MY KIDS TO KNOW WHO THE MYSTERIOUS S.J. SCOTT IS... 178

COMPOUND INTEREST AND COMPOUND ABUNDANCE.................. 180

VALUE YOUR BUSINESS THE "CHOOSE YOURSELF!" WAY: THE SECRET OF

ABUNDANCE 183

BUT HOW DO YOU VALUE A COMPANY? 186

THE ZERO TO ONE APPROACH... 188

MONOPOLY 188

SCALABILITY... 191

NETWORK EFFECT 192

BRAND 192

DEMOGRAPHICS 193

THE THREE D'S MODEL.. 194

THE THREE P'S MODEL 195

PART 3

KEEP AND GROW THE MONEY YOU MAKE 203

THE MYTHS WE'VE ALL BEEN TOLD................................... 204

HOW TO AVOID THE GREAT FINANCIAL SCAM OF THE TWENTY-FIRST

CENTURY... 208

STOP PAYING YOUR DEBTS.. 216

THE TEN MOST IMPORTANT RULES YOU NEED TO KNOW ABOUT

INVESTING 232

WHAT DO I DO WITH MY OWN MONEY?............................... 234

LESSONS LEARNED FROM DAY TRADING.............................. 238

STREET SMARTS ARE VITAL: MENTAL MODELS WORTH LEARNING 242

FOUR THINGS I DO THAT CAN CHANGE YOUR LIFE IN THE NEXT

TEN MINUTES 247

HOW TO GET AN MBA FROM EMINEM 251

AVOID REGRETS 258

HOW TO RUN A "CHOOSE YOURSELF" MEETUP......................... 264

ABOUT THE AUTHOR... 273

OTHER BOOKS BY JAMES ALTUCHER................................. 274

CONNECT WITH JAMES.. 275

INTRODUCTION:
IDEAS ARE THE CURRENCY OF THE
TWENTY-FIRST CENTURY

Ninety percent of the feedback I got about my last book, *Choose Yourself!*, had people asking for one thing: how to bridge harsh reality with the world of imagination. That is, how to become an Idea Machine. It wasn't an easy process for me. For my whole life I felt like a stray dog, dashing around until I could survive in the jungle. I was dead on the ground. I was broke. I was separated. I was fired. I was scared and lonely. Everywhere I looked, I couldn't believe people knew how to smile. They were faking it, I thought. It took a long time for me to get it—but now I get it.

In *Choose Yourself!* I describe the first tiny steps I took to get off the ground. Well, actually, the second, because the first were horribly embarrassing: I pretended to be a psychic on Craigslist just so I could make friends. But let's ignore that. I was lonely and just needed to reach out into space. Specifically, my second step was that I tried to improve physically, emotionally, mentally, and spiritually, just a little bit each day. I followed the one percent rule: improve one percent each day, in each of these areas of life.

They are all equally important. If you sit on a four-legged chair, you are firm on the ground. Use a three-legged chair, and a strong wind will blow you over. Any less than that, you'll fall easily.

Something I realized during this process: ideas are the most valuable currency of our time. *Nothing* else. Which is why in this book I focus a lot more on ideas, for example:

- Why ideas are the new currency of the twenty-first century, a century already defined by declining currencies and more volatile employment.
- Why ideas are so closely linked to wealth.
- How to create good ideas and sell them and negotiate the highest value for them.

- How to avoid other people's bad ideas.
- *Most important:* You don't need to start a business to have great ideas and create abundance.

This is not a self-help book. It's just exactly what I did for myself. I know it worked for me. I had ideas first, wealth second. It *only* worked in that order.

At my worst moments, I had no ideas. All I could do was work on others' ideas, even bad ideas, because I needed a paycheck. Then I had bad ideas. But bad ideas come back at you with loan shark prices, and you have to pay. Good ideas are a link between the real world and the world of myths and dreams. I needed to survive. I needed to pay for my family. I was going through a divorce. I was dating people who were not so good for me. I was miserable all the time, and I was scared it was going to get worse. Often there is no bottom until you make the active effort to climb out of the hole. I did that by keeping my health up and being only around people who loved me and whom I loved. That is when I created the idea matrix (see figure 1). This is when I finally took the red pill instead of the blue pill. And ever since, my life has changed 100 percent every six months. I can't even believe the ways in which it has changed. But at least I'm not crying on the floor anymore, pretending to be a psychic.

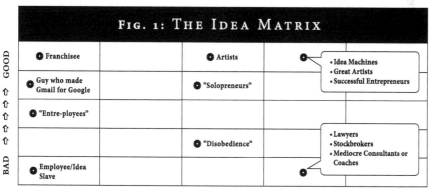

FIG. 1: THE IDEA MATRIX

	GOOD ⇧ ⇧ ⇧ ⇧ ⇧ BAD			
• Franchisee		• Artists		• Idea Machines • Great Artists • Successful Entrepreneurs
• Guy who made Gmail for Google		• "Solopreneurs"		
• "Entre-ployees"				
		• "Disobedience"		• Lawyers • Stockbrokers • Mediocre Consultants or Coaches
• Employee/Idea Slave				

WORKING ON OTHER PEOPLE'S IDEAS ⇨ ⇨ ⇨ ⇨ ⇨ GIVING OTHER PEOPLE GOOD IDEAS

The horizontal axis of the idea matrix starts off when you are working solely on others' ideas. This is not necessarily bad, but it basically means you are an employee and an idea slave to someone else's whims. You could get fired. Your boss could have bad ideas and go broke. There is no loyalty. You are not in control. You feel "stuck" all the time.

But as you keep moving toward the right on this axis, you start offering your ideas to others. At first this just helps you, but as you keep giving and giving better ideas, they start to help other people as well, and toward the end of the horizontal axis you are helping an enormous number of people.

The vertical axis of the matrix shows the quantity and quality of the ideas you are coming up with every day. It starts at zero, meaning you are not yet exercising your idea muscle, and it gets stronger as you start coming up with ten ideas a day, using something I call Idea Sex (a concept I'll describe in more detail later), and ultimately becoming an Idea Machine.

The top right of the matrix (figure 2) is when you are an Idea Machine: you are working nonstop on your own excellent ideas that help the lives of others. You mind dips into dreams, and you make them reality or art or abundance.

Founder of PayPal and first investor in Facebook Peter Thiel underlined this for me when he told me the story of Facebook founder Mark Zuckerberg turning down Yahoo's offer of $1 billion to buy his company in July of 2006. Zuckerberg would've made $250 million that summer. Thiel, who was advising Zuckerberg at the time, wanted him to take it, or at least consider accepting the offer. Zuckerberg decided in ten minutes: No. As Peter put it, ideas were more valuable to Mark than money.

FIG. 2: THE IDEA MATRIX

GOOD / BAD				
GOOD	● Franchisee		● Artists	**TOP RIGHT**
⇧	● Guy who made Gmail for Google		● "Solopreneurs"	
⇧ ⇧ ⇧ ⇧ ⇧	● "Entre-ployees"			
			● "Disobedience"	• Lawyers • Stockbrokers • Mediocre Consultants or Coaches
BAD	● Employee/Idea Slave			●

WORKING ON OTHER PEOPLE'S IDEAS ⇨ ⇨ ⇨ ⇨ ⇨ GIVING OTHER PEOPLE GOOD IDEAS

Not everyone is going to create Facebook. I never will. But everyone could create abundance in this upper right corner, and enjoys wealth as a side effect of being an Idea Machine.

The bottom left corner (figure 3): I've been here many times. For example, when I was working a job where I'd keep my office door locked all day long. I had to write an instruction manual for some chip, and I was horrible at it. I make grammar mistakes all the time, and I was worse then. My boss even called me into his office and yelled at me, "Don't you take any pride in your work?"

I'd leave work at 4:45 on the dot every day so I could hitchhike home. I wrote horrible novels at night. I hung out with my friends. I lived with a woman I didn't love. Nothing was going well. I was an idea slave. Many employees are at the bottom left of the matrix. They get their paycheck working nine to five, or longer—working on the bad ideas of others.

This is not a natural state for human beings. We *need* to explore. We're curious. We want to adapt constantly to new environments and use the part of our brain that evolved specifically so we could create new works of art or new productions. But a century of corporatism has fooled us into thinking that if we just pay our dues and climb the ladder, we'll find a pot of gold at the end. Such loyalty on behalf of companies toward employees never existed and is now gone forever as people slowly adapt to a new world.

The bottom right corner (figure 4) is where you have bad ideas that you are giving to others. Many professions exist here: lawyers and stockbrokers are the most common. They have tons of ideas—usually bad ones.

FIG. 4: THE IDEA MATRIX			
● Franchisee		● Artists	● • Idea Machines • Great Artists
● Guy who made Gmail for Google		● "Solopreneurs"	• Successful Entrepreneurs
● "Entre-ployees"			
		● "Disobedience"	BOTTOM RIGHT
● Employee/Idea Slave			

GOOD ⇧ ⇧ ⇧ ⇧ ⇧ BAD

WORKING ON OTHER PEOPLE'S IDEAS ⇨ ⇨ ⇨ ⇨ ⇨ GIVING OTHER PEOPLE GOOD IDEAS

This is not such a horrible thing for society. But it requires that the customers be aware of these professionals' hidden agendas—the fees, being charged by the hour, etc. Not all lawyers and brokers are bad. But their job is to give you a ton of ideas and hope for the best. I was mostly in this category when I acted as a consultant for companies trying to figure out what to do with their websites. Lots of ideas, most of them bad—but I needed the client to say yes so I could charge for more websites. Getting HBO to pay $75,000 for a three-page website about Dennis Miller was my crowning achievement as a bottom-righter.

At the top left (figure 5) is when you are working on good ideas, but they are based off of other people's ideas. Whoever created Gmail on top of Google is in this category. Whoever buys a losing business and turns it around is here. There is money here, just not as much as the *upper right.*

FIG. 5: THE IDEA MATRIX			
	TOP LEFT	● Artists	● • Idea Machines • Great Artists • Successful Entrepreneurs
		● "Solopreneurs"	
● "Entre-ployees"			
		● "Disobedience"	• Lawyers • Stockbrokers • Mediocre Consultants or Coaches
● Employee/Idea Slave			●

GOOD ⇧ ⇧ ⇧ ⇧ ⇧ BAD

WORKING ON OTHER PEOPLE'S IDEAS ⇨ ⇨ ⇨ ⇨ ⇨ GIVING OTHER PEOPLE GOOD IDEAS

I was in this category when I worked at HBO. I was initially hired to do some basic computer programming for them (idea slave), but then I started pitching them ideas for their website. I was still under their umbrella but I was able to become an "entre-ployee" by working on good ideas within the umbrella idea of "HBO." I made more money this way, had some fun, and got some promotions—but I was still an employee.

See in *the middle* where it says "disobedience" (figure 6)?
I don't mean like a kid running away from home for the first time. Because the kid always comes back. *I* came back. Again and again.

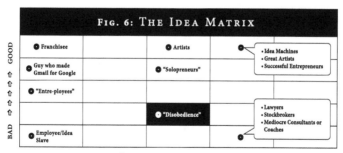

FIG. 6: THE IDEA MATRIX			
● Franchisee		● Artists	● • Idea Machines • Great Artists • Successful Entrepreneurs
● Guy who made Gmail for Google		● "Solopreneurs"	
● "Entre-ployees"			
		● "Disobedience"	• Lawyers • Stockbrokers • Mediocre Consultants or Coaches
● Employee/Idea Slave			●

GOOD ⇧ ⇧ ⇧ ⇧ ⇧ BAD

WORKING ON OTHER PEOPLE'S IDEAS ⇨ ⇨ ⇨ ⇨ ⇨ GIVING OTHER PEOPLE GOOD IDEAS

This is where you break free from the system. Where you realize that everything is a stage set and now it's time to get to work. This is where you do what you want, and say "sorry" instead of asking for permission. This is where you wake up and everyone's attached to a tube and you pull the tube out and maybe then, just like in the movies, you learn karate and fall in love.

<u>When you are in the Idea Machine, nothing can stop you.</u>

This is where abundance is. This is where seeds are planted. This is where you dip into other dimensions not yet created.

A few months ago I sent Amazon a list: ten ideas for the company to improve its self-publishing division. The folks at Amazon liked the list. They flew me out to their offices, gave me a tour of the different departments, and showed me what they were working on. It was a lot of fun. I even took a photo of the very first Starbucks, in Seattle.

They didn't pay me, but I got to meet everyone, and be at the center of the universe for publishing. And I planted a seed. Who knows where those seeds will grow in the future and what kind of abundance they'll create?

The top-righter idea machine plants lots of seeds. An idea-machine person builds many bridges into the world of dreams. I know, I hear you: you still have to pay the bills. So I'll tell you that I've also made a lot of money in this area.

One time I had a set of recommendations for a company. The company's leadership invited me to join the board of directors, where I ended up making a lot of money as my ideas were implemented. This has happened to me many times. Just yesterday I was talking to someone and gave him five ideas for how he could build a substantial business. I didn't mention my involvement at all in this market sector. But if he pursues the ideas and does well, I'll do well. It always works out this way. I try to plant seeds every day.

What about big companies like Facebook or Apple? Are they in this quadrant? Of course! Facebook is a great example: they set up the platform so that everyone can aggregate information about their identity into one place. They basically generate nonstop ideas for a billion different people around the world who want to communicate and share their online identities. Despite all the complaints you read in the media, everyone I know uses Facebook, including the people making the complaints.

My wife, Claudia, recently asked me where Marcus Lemonis, who stars in the TV show *The Profit* and who recently joined me on my podcast, would be on this matrix. Two places: He buys declining/failing businesses and helps turn them around, which is in the *top left:* take an idea from someone else and start to throw good ideas at it.

But he's also in the *top right.* He's an Idea Machine. He takes his simple concept of turning around companies, applies it to *many* companies—and now he's making a TV show out of it. He gets 40,000 e-mails from businesses each week asking for help. What a way to guarantee he has nonstop opportunities! Where are you on this matrix right now? Where can you be in six months? Who do you know that is an Idea Machine?

When I was a kid, I thought my dad was an Idea Machine. I looked up to him. No matter what the problem, he had a solution. If I argued back, he'd show me where I was wrong. And I was always wrong. He built up a good business and went public. But then it went bankrupt, he went broke, he got depressed, and he let that stop him. I don't know if he ever had a good idea again. At my worst moments I thought I was turning into him. I would cry to therapists that I was turning into him—someone who would sit all day and do nothing until he died. They would assure me, for two hundred dollars an hour, that I wasn't. But how could they know?

The Daily Practice I discuss throughout this book gives me the energy to come up with ideas, and to come up with ideas for coming up with ideas. I write down ten ideas a day no matter what.

Being scared and lonely happens in a cycle. It affects all of us. Watching the river go into the ocean sparks a little bit of that loneliness. But I think we're *meant* to often feel lonely and scared. It allows us to recalibrate where we are and ask the important question, is *this* what I'm supposed to be doing right now? When I am filled with fear is *exactly* the time when I want my idea muscle humming, when I *must* write those ten ideas a day down and become an Idea Machine.

It's when I'm most scared that I get out of bed and I know that today is the day I can do anything I want to.

It's not an affirmation. Or wishful thinking. Or the words of a song.

It's a box I check when I'm done writing my ideas down.

KA-BOOM!

THE 18 NEW RULES OF ABUNDANCE

ABS: Always Be Selling (both in a presentation and via copywriting)

ABN: Always Be Negotiating (which means win-win, not war)

The **Idea Muscle Rule** (take out a pad, write down a list of ideas, every day)

- **The Real Rules of Leadership** (give more to others than you expect back for yourself)

- **How to Live by Themes Instead of Goals** (goals will break your heart)

- **The Reinvention Manifesto** (which will happen repeatedly throughout a life)

- **The Entrepreneur Rule.** Not everyone is an entrepreneur, but learning these rules of entrepreneurship will help you choose yourself instead of letting others choose you. It's this mastery over the gatekeepers that leads to the greatest successes.

- **The Monopoly Rule.** Nobody can predict what will happen. But understanding demographic trends and how to use them to take advantage of the coming monopolies in society will be of great benefit.

- **Idea Sex** (get good at coming up with ideas. Then combine them. Master the intersection)

- **The 1% Rule** (every week try to get better 1% physically, emotionally, mentally)

- **The Google Rule** - give constantly to the people in your network. The value of your network increases linearly if you get to know more people, but EXPONENTIALLY if the people you know, get to know and help each other. Note that Google measures its success by how quickly it sends you to other websites where you can help. But then…where do you return to when you need more help?…Google.

- **Failure is a Myth:** how to fail so that a failure turns into a new beginning. Turn the word "failure" into "experiment". Become the scientist of your life, the explorer of your future.

- **The $2 Bill Rule:** simple tools to increase productivity

- **The Secrets of Mastery.** You can't learn this in school with each "field" being regimented into equal 50-minute periods. Mastery begins when formal education ends. Find the topic that sets your heart on fire. Then combust.

- **The Noise Rule:** news, advice books, fees upon fees in almost every area of life. Create your own noise instead of falling in line with the others.

- **The "Save Big Rule".** Don't save small. Save big. Big is a worthless college degree. Big is a house. Saving 10 cents on a cup of coffee is a poor man's way to get rich. There is a myth that "saving a dollar is the same as making a dollar". This simply is not true. It ignores the fact that you start off with money. If you start off with $100 you can ONLY save $100 but you can MAKE a gazillion dollars.

- **Investing is a Tax on the Middle Class.** There are exceptions, which I'll show in the chapter "The Ultimate Guide to Investing".

- **The Daily Practice.** Discussed in *Choose Yourself!* but I'll describe a little more here and the science behind it.

In the chapters that follow I'll dive deep on these rules and how I've used them.

Society is very good at keeping the carrot at the end of the stick that it puts in front of our face. It then says, "hurry" and "get that carrot".

But the key is that success is found only by avoiding the carrot, ignoring it, choosing yourself for peace, for abundance, for gratitude, in that order.

If you do all this you will gradually make more and more money and help more and more people. At least, I've seen it happen for me and for others.

How I Ended Up in Prison—And How I Broke Out

I spent at least thirty years of my life in prison. I tried to break out several times and was punished. Finally I freed myself. In this book you will read about how I broke out of prison. My previous book, *Choose Yourself!*, gave the basics of how you can free yourself—how to get physically, emotionally, mentally, and spiritually healthy.

This book takes it one step further and reveals what I've done to create actual abundance for myself—to turn my life around in ways that still surprise me. To change my life completely, still, every six months.

But how did I get in prison in the first place? What kind of prison am I even talking about? Who else is there with me? Are you?

It happened on the first day of nursery school. I was put in handcuffs and led out to the car. Sort of. In reality, I asked my dad what was happening. Why did I have to go to school? Every word out of his mouth was a lie that kept me in prison for decades.

He said, "Well, first you have two years of nursery school. Then a year of kindergarten, then you have twelve years of grade school and high school. Then you go to college for four years. Then you might get a master's degree and become a lawyer or you might go to medical school and become a doctor, then you work for forty years, get promoted if you do a good job, make some money. And then, when you are as old as Grandpa, you can retire.

"And during that time," he continued, "you buy a house, you get married and have kids and send them to college. And then they do the same thing."

I thought about Grandpa. He was so old. He could barely walk. He had heart attacks every other year. He sat in front of his old TV and did crossword puzzles. He couldn't move fast enough to chase after me.

It's not my father's fault that he said all of these things. He was just repeating to me the life he was leading—the life that *his* father had taught him to lead. My friends all said the same thing. Not in nursery school, but in grade school, and in college, and at my first couple of jobs where maybe a dozen of us would vie for the same promotions when jobs opened up.

My friends, family, and colleagues also said the same thing when it was time to buy a house. It is the single biggest expense most people will ever make in their lives as a percentage of their net worth—and nobody questioned it. This is "what you do," *of course*. And not only that—you take on *massive* debt to do it.

This is what people do. This is how people live. This is what life is about. That life was a rainbow and each of these important decisions were shades on the rainbow and at the end would be the pot of gold.

So how could I question this? Of course it would be good to have a job at a great company and then put my money in a 401(k) where I would never see it again, and buy insurance products that I would never use, and buy a car, or maybe two, that I would never drive, that would contain the latest this and that and the other thing, and by the way you'll have to get a new this and that in a few years. This was all part of the American Dream. Get a checkup once a year. Get blood tests. Live your life. But protect yourself. Don't step out of the box. Take care of yourself. Life is hard. But then life is easy if you follow the rules.

I can't pinpoint whose fault it is—and it doesn't matter. If you fall down and you get hurt, you don't have to know exactly the biology of why you got hurt; you just know you're in pain, and then you do something about it.

Every time I refused to believe in and act on the American Dream, I was punished severely. Because everyone else has invested so much of their money and lives in this dream that it freaks them out when other people deviate—let alone take a detour, or be happier.

But here's the truth. At every level of the "Dream," someone is stealing from you.

First they steal from your time. Then they steal from your loves – your passions, the things you love to do, the people you love – all of it. Then they steal money from you. Oh, I should mention, they steal *a lot* of money from you. Then they steal from your middle age, where the ambition you worked for starts to marinate into meaning.

Then they steal from your retirement, where now you are so exhausted from paying off so many debts and so many needless expenses that you forgot how to live, Live, *Live.*

But I am not complaining—and neither should anyone reading this book. Why?

Because the game has completely changed.

The economists cannot explain how. The professors cannot explain how. Your colleagues and friends might not be able to explain how. But everything has changed, 100 percent, and for the better. And *now* is the critical time to take advantage of those changes.

The old ladder metaphor has shifted. There's no longer a ladder. It's more like an amusement park. And we are all invited to play in it. There's more opportunity for abundance than ever. This is the new paradigm of this century, a century where *ideas* take precedence over money in terms of creating abundance. These are the new rules. And this book will show you they work in your favor, and how you can succeed in this new economy.

A person who still follows the old way will get an education through graduate school, get a great job, get the promotions—but will at some point feel stuck, lost, may even betrayed if he is fired or unhappy or if the world didn't turn out as he had hoped it would, or if the ladder he imagined turned out to be missing a rung and he fell down, broke a leg, and had to start from scratch, slightly more broken than he was before.

A person who follows the new approach, with the new skills of abundance that I outline in this book, will skip through the ladder. He'll realize that there is no ladder anymore; there's just opportunity. He'll see that we live in a world of ideas and we can skip from one idea to another, each one building on the last, each one creating the seeds of abundance that will grow into our lives.

But the only way to take advantage of that abundance is to learn the skills, the habits, the hacks, the techniques, the tricks, the wonders of how to succeed and accomplish in this new world of innovation and freedom. In *Choose Yourself!* I describe the philosophy: if you don't make your own choices, someone else will do it for you—and it won't be pleasant. I describe how to build a Daily Practice that will lead you into a world where you actually could make the choices for yourself. But it's not that easy. There are skills to learn. There are things to do now. This book is about how to do them—and how you can *succeed in the new world*. So let's get started.

THE FACTS

LET'S LOOK AT SOME CHARTS FIRST:

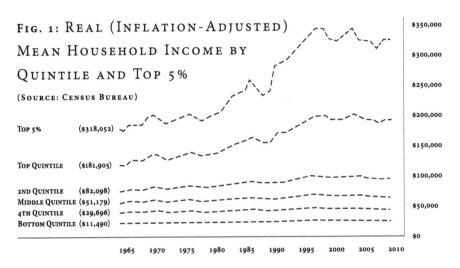

Chart from: Dshort.com

Forget the top line in figure 1. That's the richest 5 percent. We're all going to be in that line if we follow the rules of abundance. Look at the next line, and you'll notice that the average income of the bottom 50 percent of the country is basically flat. And these aren't bad incomes. The second quintile makes on average $82,000 a year. These incomes are *real*—which in economist terms means they are *adjusted for inflation*. Which is a BS term designed to fool people into thinking things are better. First off, even inflation adjusted, things are not better for 75 percent of people. They are just basically flat.

But what does the term *inflation* mean?

To be honest, I have no idea. I'm not sure anyone really does. The formula the government uses is very obscure, yet that is the number every economist uses.

But I do know what inflation does *not* include. It doesn't include the price of a home. So if home prices go up faster than inflation, then a salary will never let you buy a home better than your parent's home unless you borrow money. And the banks will certainly lend out at rates higher than inflation. What if housing doesn't go up faster than inflation? Well, they don't. The hundred-year return on housing is 0.2 percent annually. Good luck trying to get rich off that (More on that in a bit.)

Something else inflation doesn't take into account is another trap of the old way: college tuition. Let's look at another chart (figure 2).

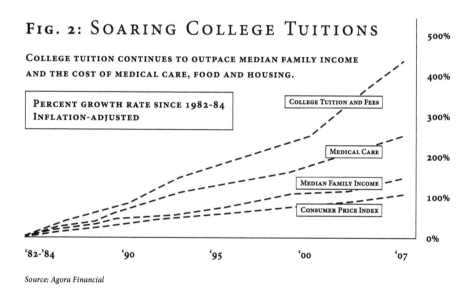

FIG. 2: SOARING COLLEGE TUITIONS

COLLEGE TUITION CONTINUES TO OUTPACE MEDIAN FAMILY INCOME AND THE COST OF MEDICAL CARE, FOOD AND HOUSING.

PERCENT GROWTH RATE SINCE 1982-84
INFLATION-ADJUSTED

COLLEGE TUITION AND FEES

MEDICAL CARE

MEDIAN FAMILY INCOME

CONSUMER PRICE INDEX

500%
400%
300%
200%
100%
0%

'82-'84   '90   '95   '00   '07

Source: Agora Financial

Both college and healthcare costs have risen faster than inflation while salaries have remained flat.

It's almost unbelievable when we put it all together. The *three biggest expenses* in a person's life—housing, college, and later on, healthcare—have all crushed the average person with their rising costs. No wonder society as a whole is so disappointed in where we are.

But don't worry if you've already paid for an education. Or paid for a home. Or are in great debt. It's simply important to have a clear windshield while we drive forward in the rain. It's important to keep the above facts in mind as we begin our in-depth dive into the new rules of abundance.

The History of the End of the World

I'm not a historian or an economist. I don't read the news. I don't follow up on the latest in climate change or World War III (the combined fronts in Syria, Israel, Iraq, Afghanistan, Ukraine, etc.) When people ask me about current events, they are sometimes shocked that I have no idea what they are talking about.

I mean, it's definitely sad. I wouldn't wish those tragedies on anyone. If I wanted to, I could cry all day. But I don't want to do that. I know the best thing I can do is exactly what I'm doing. We all have our ways of helping people. Most of us wake up in the morning and wish we could do our best and be honest and try to make the world a better place.

I'm convinced that if I follow the Daily Practice I outline extensively in my book *Choose Yourself!* (and later in this book), then it won't just be me who reaps benefits, but also everyone else.

When *Choose Yourself!* first came out, someone close to my wife said, "I refuse to read it. The title sounds selfish." My wife started to respond and then thought better of it. Why bother? She knew she wasn't going to change his mind. And the guy was just saying this to provoke a response. Often someone who is trying to provoke an argument is really engaging in what I call "status junk-food binging." For evolutionary reasons we all try to find out where we belong on the status hierarchy. That's how we've survived as mammals for millions of years. That's one of the key ingredients that separate a mammal from a reptile. A reptile gets born and then hops on his way. He already knows how to take care of himself and he gets down to business. He doesn't really care about status. He cares about survival.

Mammals care about survival, too, but they know their chances of surviving increase if they travel in a pack, a herd, a tribe, a city, a state, a kingdom, an empire, or whatever you want to call it. And inside the tribe, each mammal figures out where it is in line for food and for mates. This is neither good nor bad. It's not like any ape says, "I wish I were higher in the status hierarchy."

I'm not saying that you should be a lower-status ape. This is just a fact of our having been mammals for millions of years: your brain is going to spend a lot of time figuring where you are in the hierarchy. Then it's going to govern your behavior, often without your conscious permission, based on where it concludes you belong. The only way a mammal can choose itself is by fighting a mammal above it in the hierarchy and winning, even if this means maiming or killing.

So when you see a human trying to pick a fight, it's really just a primitive form of this status clinging. They The person feels that their status is not high enough, so they will attempt to control things by picking what they view as an easy fight. So you can fight and I can ignore—because humans, unlike any other species, *can choose*. We get to *pick* the hierarchy in which we want to find status. No other species gets to make this choice.

Everyone who lives according to the old way has doubtlessly noticed this: you work at a company and a job opens up , and there is a ferocious fight to see who is going to get promoted internally to fill that position. It involves maybe a tiny increase in salary and almost always a huge increase in work—but people will kill for that move up in status.

And then let's say you leave that workplace, and you are suddenly very confused: why was I ever trying to get that job? Look at how much bigger the world is now. Look at how much sunnier everything seems.

I ask people for testimonials and stories about how *Choose Yourself!* helped them. I get e-mails, phone calls, even people stopping me on the street to tell me how they quit their jobs and it took a few weeks/months/year but now things are better than ever. And it all happens when they start doing the Daily Practice I'm about to summarize for you.

We get to choose the sandbox we want to play in. We get to choose the hierarchy where we are going to fight for improvement. How come? Because our brains are bigger than those of reptiles. That's it.

We developed a prefrontal cortex for this exact reason. Well, almost. It was really evolved so we could travel. We were nomadic and we were growing and soon East Africa was no longer big enough for our species. So we went to Europe. We crossed over Asia. We even crossed a massive body of water to get to Australia. We went to cold areas, hot areas, jungles, deserts, etc. and had to learn how to adapt and survive. Our brains evolved to handle this immense adaptation.

And now we can use it our brains to adapt to different social hierarchies. We are still status-seeking machines—,; - there's no way to escape millions of years of genetic programming. But we can choose the exact circumstances in which we want to define our status in.

The history of the world, in the traditional sense, is over. I'm not saying this to promote fearmongering, but just throw out the history textbooks for a second. You may well have heard the phrase "history is written by the winners." The only problem is, what if the authors of history are about to become losers? They will have no idea! They wrote all the history books!

So in a thousand words or so, I'm going to give you the history of the last hundred years, and you can start to see what is about to happen.

I can start with any point in history, really, but I will start a century ago to the day that I'm writing this chapter: June 28, 1914, and the assassination of Archduke Ferdinand that kicked off World War I. And a relatively minor country on the other side of the Atlantic that had pretty much kept to itself until now became the only superpower left in the world: the United States. Everyone was in debt to us and we now had the largest navy for the first time. If you control the water, which covers most of the planet, you control the planet.

Then non-Germany Europe destroyed the German economy with reparations, which in turn brought down the European economy and led to the rise of Nazism throughout Germany. The European economy spread to the United States, causing the Great Depression. The Depression and general worldwide economic collapse led to World War II.

BOOM!

Guess what happened that then changed everything for the next seventy years, ultimately leading to total economic collapse in the United States? Little boys put on helmets and got real guns and left the country in order to shoot other little boys.

And while the little boys played, women went to work. When the men got back, the women, quite correctly, didn't want to go home. They liked working and making money! So we got the first taste of the double-income family. They had more money and they wanted to spend it.

Let's buy a house and a fence. Let's buy two cars. Let's buy a TV! And a phone. And a pool if we want! It felt good to spend money. It made us happy to buy a new toy. The toys have pretty much remained the same. They just got bigger and better and faster and, in some cases, more expensive. But then the happiness wears off after a while: you have to buy a new toy. And a new one.

So, we needed more money.

The 1960s started a new stock market boom but it wasn't enough. Lyndon Johnson pumped the economy full of dollars with his "Great Society" program and he also increased spending on defense (or, really, offensive spending) when we went to Vietnam. But then we needed more money to afford *that*. So Nixon took us off the gold standard, so the dollar could wander off where it will.

Here's what happens when inflation occurs. It's not a bad thing at first. Nobody really knows its inflation. The first thing you notice is that you have more money. Inflation makes you feel flush at first.

So suddenly everyone felt flush until prices started to rise too quickly in the 1970s. Then we felt sick again—which meant that we needed more money to pay for the price increases.

Enter the '80s junk bond boom. Creative ways were found to basically create money out of nothing. And this fueled a stock market boom. We had more money!

When this started to slow down (stock market crash, people going to jail, etc.), thank god the Soviet Union collapsed. Peace dividend!

But then recession again in 1993–94. Hmmm… What could we do now? Internet stock market boom. Suddenly, everything would cost nothing (since it's all digital!) and there were no taxes on Internet sales. So Wall Street took every company public, creating enormous paper wealth. The Federal Reserve helped out by pretending to be nervous about Y2K and printing an enormous amount of money to keep things going, which led to a housing boom. Then Wall Street joined in by coming up with creative ways to bundle the housing loans to create more paper wealth for everyone.

I have no political agenda in saying this. Nor am I blaming anyone. Everyone was looking out for their own interests: the spenders on Main Street, the government, Wall Street, and all the bureaucrats, lobbyists, bloated corporations, media, and everybody in between. It all collapsed for about a five-month period, until the US government once again printed up trillions of dollars to stabilize things. And that's the end.

This is the final bubble. The US government now has to keep printing money to keep things stable. Maybe when the economy booms again they can hold off—but that might be a while.

This is why we can't rely on anything to bail us out anymore. There's nothing left, unless you're getting a direct check from the government, the bailer of last resort. I see it from my vantage point. I'm invested in about thirty companies. And I'm on the boards of several others, including a billion-revenues company in the employment sector. Basically, people's salaries are going down versus inflation, versus healthcare costs, versus housing costs, versus everything. A salary will not keep your family afloat. Two salaries won't even keep your family afloat.

You have to master the rules taught in this book. You have to learn how to live in the new economy.

There is no single style of business that works for everyone. If it were that easy, then there would be too much competition and there will be no money left. I do know that when I began living by the *idea matrix principles of abundance* outlined in these pages, they worked for me and they began working for the people I described them to. Some people quit their jobs and are now making a steadily rising income doing that they love. And others got wealthy.

True wealth occurs when you don't have to bow down to any gatekeepers—regardless of the money involved. Money is just a by-product. You are out of prison. You are free.

But why do I feel so strongly about encouraging people choose themselves?

Well, one reason is that I enjoy writing. Another is that I want to help people because I get so many e-mails from people in despair. And another part is that I think we *all* benefit when one of us benefits. Not everyone will read this book. And initially, only a few who are on the various lists I've shared this book with. The more people who choose themselves, the more people we can all do business with, the more people will focus on the actual problems in society instead of the fictional ones the news proposes every news cycle, every twenty-four hours.

If you choose to follow the new ideas presented here, you will gradually make more and more money and help more and more people. I've seen it happen for myself and for others.

Don't plagiarize the lives of your parents, your peers, your teachers, your colleagues, and your bosses. Be the criminal of their rules. Create your own life.

I wish I were you because if you follow the above, then you will most likely end up doing what you love and getting massively rich while helping many others. I didn't do that when I was twenty. But now, at forty-six, I'm really grateful I have the chance every day to wake up and improve one percent.

OK—let's' choose ourselves for wealth.

———⌘———

WHY ALL THE PERSONAL FINANCE GURUS ARE OUT OF DATE

P erhaps you found this book in the personal finance section of a store or website. The phrase "personal finance" was never a thing before 1970, give or take a few years. Here's what people expected—and in many cases at that time, they were correct.

We've already discussed the pattern pretty much everyone followed: Go to school. Go to college. Make connections in college. Get a job as junior associate of sales at big company. Start placing 10 percent of your income in imaginary structures set up by a partnership between the government and banks called IRAs and Roth IRAs and 401(k)s and other structures.

Get promotions. Watch the stock market go up. Watch the value of your house go up. Now you are a VP (or even higher!). Then, retire at sixty-five with enough money saved, combined with Social Security, to take you well into your eighties, where you can die in peace.

Of course, there could be some blips along the way. Maybe you get divorced. Maybe you get fired or get hired by a new firm. But the blips were not incredibly drastic. Let's call this timeline the "Ladder of success."

Never before in the 2 million years of humanity's history was there a ladder of success. But after the post–World War II boom of prosperity in the United States we now had many decisions to make:

- When is the right time to buy a house?
- How important is it to go to college?
- How do I manage assets for tax purposes (and if needed, divorce purposes)?
- How do I save for "retirement" (that period between the Rolex watch party and a grave being dug for you by your closest loved ones).
- How to set reasonable goals for different ages so you know you are on the right track.

- How to best function in your particular career track so as to maximize your chances of rising up the ladder of success to the highest point possible given your skills and talents.

- How to best fit into the cog of the enormous productivity machine that America was becoming so you can aspire to take advantage of the many opportunities.

- How to protect your assets (estate planning) so that your kids and their kids have a decent chance at continuing any legacy you might leave.

- When is it good to go into debt? And once in debt, what is a good debt reduction plan?

- What's the role of inflation and how do you protect yourself against it so that it doesn't eat into savings?

- How to keep track of everything in a convenient place (ledgers, software, etc.). And even

- How to define how much risk you can take, given your age, your income, your assets, and given that you have a certain level of allowed risk, how to take advantage of that risk to maybe invest differently based on the statistics accumulated over a relatively short period of human history.

Entire industries were set up to answer each one of these questions. In fact, I would go so far as to say that every single one of these questions is *still* being addressed by multibillion-dollar industries—in some cases, even multitrillion-dollar industries. And these industries sometimes make mistakes (the 2008 financial meltdown, the 2000 IPO bubble, the Asian crisis of 1997, the savings and loan corruption of the late '80s and early '90s, and so on).

In some cases, these industries have been very successful. I am not going to call out any names. But many people made tens of millions of dollars writing books, having TV shows, creating software, giving advice, and creating companies that have attempted to answer the above questions and focused on one question or other.

This was, and is, "personal finance."

As noted, the phrase "personal finance" didn't exist before 1970. Nor will that phrase have any meaning in the near future. The world has already changed, but momentum has kept the personal finance industries alive and media outlets from TV networks to book publishers have kept alive the myth that you need this help in order to make the best decisions for your life. The reason I separated the points above is that every item involves a fee.

For instance, there is a cost if you go to college. When you buy a house, there is a cost. When you decide to stay in a job for a long time, there is a cost. When you make financial decisions with a bank, and then a financial planner, and then a mutual fund, there are costs and fees at every level.

It's common sense that there is, and should be, a cost for all of these things. And in many cases, you get benefits for that cost. That's why people pay. But now the benefits are getting fewer and fewer, and even turning from benefits into drawbacks. But many people—millions, even—don't want to hear about this. They think and want to think that the same rules still apply, and so they squeeze tight their prison door so nobody from outside can open it, even though there are no locks.

When I write about these topics it's not like people just ignore me. The idea that the economy has completely changed and that the old way won't work anymore actually gets people *angry*. I've had many death threats. I've had many people who can't handle the changes that have happened write me and tell me I don't know what I'm talking about.

But why do people get so angry? If they disagree with me—which they clearly do—why not just ignore me?

Again, with each aspect of "personal finance" (and I'm going to keep putting it in quotes) there is a cost—sometimes a significant cost. Sometimes the cost is so large that your entire life changes forever because of it. When something has a large cost, as all the decisions in personal finance often do, a cognitive bias called "investment bias" kicks in.

A cognitive bias occurs when our brains—in their well-intentioned attempts to protect us from the wild—keep us on the narrow path that has been deemed safe for various reasons. Some of those reasons are genetic. Some of them are due to the habits you've developed during your life. Some of them come from the company you keep (your "tribe"), and some of them come from people whom you admire.

When an event that challenges your cognitive bias occurs, a neurochemical called cortisol shoots all over your brain. This is the same chemical that would get you to run as fast as you could a million years ago if you saw a lion. Of course, there are no lions chasing you in the streets anymore—but your brain doesn't know that,

Today's version of the lion sighting might be someone telling you that you made a decision at too great a cost to you. Then your investment bias kicks in and your brain freaks out. *No! Run!*

This is why this book is not for everyone. If you tell someone they made a mistake in buying a house, even now, seven years after the housing bubble burst, they might go crazy. If you tell someone that college might not be the best use of four years of their life and $100,000 of their money at such a young age, they might go insane thinking about what you are suggesting—especially if they've already invested the time and money and need to push away any feelings of regret.

If you tell someone that getting a job and a salary might not be the best way to make money, in fact it might be the best way to go broke, this doesn't even compute. The investment bias is too large. "This is my entire life you're talking about!"

This is also why I ask that you not give this book to anyone. Just put it aside. Maybe later you can take it out while you are in the bathroom and open up to one of the middle chapters and see what you think. If you don't like what you read, you can use it as toilet paper.

The key point to remember: every level of personal finance has a fee, or cost.

Those costs add up to millions of dollars over the course of a lifetime, sometimes over the course of just a few years. They are so great—and spread over so many households in our economy—that they are often the difference between wealth and insolvency. The net societal result is an increase in inflation, which continues the vicious cycle of personal finance all over again.

This is why it's time to get out of that cycle. It's time to embrace and being living according to the new rules set forth in this book.

Throughout this book, I talk about abundance, which often means money. And for the most part in this book you can assume it means money.

But consider as well that abundance means gratitude. You can't be grateful for things you don't have an abundance of. I'm abundant in children so I'm grateful. I'm abundant in friends so I'm grateful. When I'm stuck in traffic, I'm abundant in time where I can sit and listen to music and think and daydream. I'm also grateful I live in an area that so many people want to live in.

Abundance means many things. This book explains how I try to create abundance in every area of my life. Money is just a side effect of real abundance. Sometimes I fail miserably at creating money. But as long as my abundance continues to grow, all of the side effects of abundance will.

⸙

Develop a Practice for Success

I know you've heard this before, but it's important to emphasize it again: the only way to have success is to build the foundation for it.

I've failed so many times it's almost like I'm a one-man statistical experiment on failure. So I finally took a step back and asked, what was I doing *right* on the way up, and what was I doing *wrong* on the way down?

Four common themes that always arose. My "four bodies"—physical, emotional, mental, and spiritual—were working for me.

One time I made a lot of money and I thought, "OK, now I'm done. I don't need to do all the right things anymore." Two years later I was dead broke.

If you start hanging around with people who don't love and support you, then you'll die. If you don't take care of your body, then you'll die. If you don't exercise your idea muscle (a major topic of this book), then you'll die. If you complain instead of feel gratitude for the bounty in your life, then you'll waste your life (I don't say "you'll die" here, but you will live a miserable life).

My *only* three goals in life are

1. To be happy.
2. To eradicate unhappiness in my life.
3. For every day to be as smooth as possible. No hassles.

That's it. I'm not asking for much. I need simple goals, *or else* I can't achieve them.

There have been at least ten times in my life that everything seemed so low I felt like I would never achieve the above three things and the world would be better off without me. Other times I felt like I was stuck at a crossroads and would never figure out which road to take. Each time I bounced back.

The Daily Practice is to take care of these four areas of your life every single day without fail. It doesn't mean you have to go crazy with them, just a tiny bit: aim for a one percent improvement a day.

But wait! you're thinking. This is supposed to be a book on wealth. Well, how do you ever expect to get there if you don't start taking care of your basic needs? The old way is to concern yourself solely with making money. The new way requires that you see how everything in your life is connected, including the physical, emotional, mental, and spiritual.

PHYSICAL

- Sleep well.
- Eat well.
- Exercise. This doesn't mean go to the power gym with a trainer. It might just mean take a walk three times a week. Whatever works for you.

EMOTIONAL

- Be around people who love and support you and whom you love and support.
- Ignore everyone else as much as you can. Engage with nobody who is bad to you. When you get in the mud with a pig, the pig gets happy and you get dirty.

MENTAL

I discuss this more in the chapter on becoming an Idea Machine. But basically, the idea muscle atrophies if you don't use it every day. Every single day write down ten ideas.

SPIRITUAL

There's a saying, "Complaining is draining."

Whenever you notice you are complaining or anxious or nervous or scared, try to stop yourself and do two things:

1. Repeat to yourself, "I notice I'm feeling anxious." This distances you from the feeling of "I'm anxious!"
2. Think of at least one new thing you are grateful for.

Results of the Daily Practice

Within about one month of beginning the practice, I started to notice coincidences happening. I started to feel lucky. People were smiling at me more.

Within three months, the ideas had really started flowing, to the point where I felt overwhelming urges to execute the ideas.

Within six months, *good* ideas had started flowing. I'd begin executing them, and everyone around me would help me put everything together.

Within a year my life was *always* (and it still is) completely different—100 percent upside down from the year before. More money, more luck, more health, etc. And then I'd get lazy and stop doing the practice. And everything would fall apart again. But now I'm trying to do it every day.

It's hard to do all of this every day. Nobody is perfect. I don't know if I'll do all of these things today. But I know when I do it, and it works.

Nobody knows how long it takes to develop a new habit. Some research says forty-five days. Some research says sixty-six days. Who knows?

Do this Daily Practice every day for six months, even just a tiny bit, and I guarantee your life will be completely different—for the better.

Part 1

NEW GAME, NEW RULES

WHAT IF YOU DON'T KNOW WHAT YOUR PASSION IS?

Y ou know by now that this book is about the new rules for abundance, and how to create it in your life. One question people ask me is, what if everyone does this?

My answer: don't worry about anybody else. As the title says, *Choose Yourself!* Choose what you love. Choose your passion.

And if you are having trouble identifying your passion? Well, it's a big world. Why limit yourself to a single passion? Here's a secret: you don't have to worry about "finding" your passion. You're naturally going to get passionate about what you are good at.

The first time I made a dollar on my own, I became passionate about delivering newspapers. If you want to break out of a rut, out of the cubicle slavery, and you're working on your idea muscle and the other aspects of the Daily Practice, then you can really go in any direction. But let me give you one starting idea to get your juices flowing.

Start what's called an "information product." There are a few billion people on the Internet and they all have credit cards (or PayPal, thank you, Peter). Remember this phrase: "Get Paid, Get Laid, Lose Weight"—because those are the three things people will pay for. I have paid for all three of those items at various points in my life in some form or other. Even though I don't need to lose weight I just bought something in that category ten minutes ago. I went to Dave Asprey's Bulletproof Coffee site and bought his ingredients for a coffee that can help metabolism, improve brainpower, etc. I had read his book, scheduled him for my podcast, and already tried some of the basic ideas he mentioned and found for myself that they worked.

For the past twenty years I've been buying financial newsletters. Some decent, some great, some not so great. But I was looking for a way to "Get Paid." I know people who make seven-figure incomes selling newsletters or webinars or other digital products in each of those categories.

Why start a newsletter or other information product? For a few reasons:

- MONOPOLY. If you have your own twist on an idea, then you've just created a niche and can dominate it before you build into other markets.
- SCALABILITY. You always make money while you sleep.
- BRAND. If you become the expert in your niche, then you're there for life. People will associate your name with the niche.

There are almost no costs to adding a new customer. Marketing is your main cost, but once you develop a good product you slowly build up by doing what is called A/B testing. You can use the chapter "How to Persuade Anyone of Anything in Ten Seconds" to come up with ideas for ads.

Test ads out on Facebook to see if people click and buy. You can buy ads super cheap. And you can use not only Facebook, but any ad network. The best networks for advertising change all the time, which makes it easy to find out what works for you. Then, when something works, scale it up. If *nothing* works, start from scratch until you find something that works. See books like *Breakthrough Advertising, The Architecture of Persuasion,* and Kevin Harrington's (from *AsSeenOnTV* and *Shark Tank*) book *Act Now,* where he discusses the power of testimonials and infomercials.

I had one friend a few years ago who lost his job as a TV show anchor. He was depressed and verging on broke. He moved to his hometown and went into virtual isolation. He finally wrote an article about stocks he thought would go up in the new economy. I told him, "You're crazy. Don't make this a free article. Sell it for two hundred dollars and call it, "One Hundred Stocks That Will Go Up 1000 percent." He *did* it and sold two thousand copies and then bought a fifty-acre farm and wrote his next ten books and newsletters.

I'm not insinuating that free is bad. In fact you want to write for free as much as possible and for as many sites as possible to build up your brand. But this friend already had a great brand (he had his own TV show!) and was ready to make some money. And guess what? He was right. Most of the stocks did go up 1000 percent.

Try the following exercise:

Come up with ten ideas you can write newsletters about. They don't have to be in the above three categories. My wife, Claudia, loves airplanes—hates flying but she loves planes. (I don't really get it, either.) But she could tell you every detail about every seat on every plane and how much you should pay for it and what else you should get and what tricks you can use to fly cheap and how to get into the first-class lounge, etc. So she could write a newsletter on travel. Not to mention write one about all the countries she's traveled to cheaply where she's both studied and taught yoga. "Yoga Travel Destinations." See how easy that was?

The old way of doing things is to not try. To think that the best course of action is to climb the corporate ladder and hope, hope, and hope that the ladder is not crooked or broken or that there isn't someone at the top that's about to throw the ladder off the building. The new way of doing things, the red pill, is to jump into the abyss. To try and fail and cry and wail until finally you say, "I can't do this one more time. I just can't. Please don't make me."

But you do it anyway. And that one last time, you chose yourself

---

Why You *Have* to Quit Your Job This Year

This was going to end badly.

My boss screamed at me in front of my colleagues. I had done something wrong, of course: I had sent a product to the client without debugging it thoroughly. It was my fault. But I don't like being yelled at. And fortunately I was sitting on a job offer that I decided to take that moment. So the next day I walked in and said the magic words: "I quit." And then a few years after that, I quit again, and never went back to work in the corporate world.

I'm going to tell you why you have to quit your job. Why you need to get the ideas moving. Why you need to build a foundation for your life or soon you will have no roof.

———— ༄ ————

THE MIDDLE CLASS IS DEAD

A few weeks ago I visited a friend of mine who manages a trillion dollars. No joke. A trillion. If I told you the name of the family he worked for you would say, "They have a trillion? Really?" But that's what happens when $10 million compounds at 2 percent over two hundred years.

He said, "Look out the windows." We looked out at all the office buildings around us. "What do you see?" he said.

"I don't know."

"They're empty! All the cubicles are empty. The middle class is being hollowed out." And I took a closer look. Entire floors were dark. Or there were floors with one or two cubicles occupied, but the rest empty. "It's all outsourced, or technology has taken over for the paper shufflers," he explained.

"Not all the news is bad," he said. "More people than ever entered the upper class last year." But, he said, more people are temp staffers than ever.

And that's the new paradigm. The middle class has died. The American Dream never really existed. It was a marketing scam. The biggest provider of mortgages for the past fifty years, Fannie Mae, had as their slogan, "We make the American Dream come true." It was just a marketing slogan all along. How many times have I cried because of a marketing slogan?

You've Been Replaced

Technology, outsourcing, a growing temp staffing industry, productivity efficiencies—these have all replaced the middle class.

Most jobs that existed twenty years ago aren't needed now. Maybe they never were needed. The entire first decade of this century was spent with CEOs in their Park Avenue clubs crying through their cigars, "How are we going to fire all this dead weight?" The year 2008 finally gave them the chance. "It was the economy!" they said. The country has been out of a recession since 2009, or for almost six years now. But the jobs have not come back. I asked many of these CEOS, "Did you just use that as an excuse to fire people?" And they would wink and say, "Let's just leave it at that."

I'm on the board of directors of a temp staffing company with $1 billion revenues. I can see it happening across every sector of the economy. Everyone is getting fired. Robots are the new middle class.

Corporations Don't Like You

The executive editor of a *major* news publication took me out to lunch to get advice on how to expand the publication's website traffic. When I say a "major news publication," I am talking major.

But before I could begin giving any sort of advice, he started complaining to me: "Our top writers keep putting their Twitter names in their posts, and then when they get more followers they start asking for raises."

"What's the problem with that?" I asked. "Don't you want popular and well-respected writers?"

He said, "No, we want to be about the news. We don't want anyone to be an individual star." In other words, his main job was to destroy the career aspirations of his most talented people, the people who swore their loyalty to him, the people who worked ninety hours a week for him. If they only worked thirty hours a week and were slightly more mediocre he would've been happy. But he wants to them stay in the hole, and will throw them a meal every once in a while in exchange for their excrement. If anyone is a reporter out there and wants to e-mail me privately, I will tell you who it was. But basically, it's all of your bosses. Every single one of them.

MONEY IS NOT HAPPINESS

A common question that I get asked at least once a week during my Twitter Q&A (every Thursday from 3:30 to 4:30 p.m. EST) is "should I take the job I like or should I take the job that pays more money?" Leaving aside the question of "should I take a job *at all*," let's talk about money for a second.

First, the science: studies show that an increase in salary only offers marginal to zero increase in "happiness" above a certain level. This is because of a basic fact: people spend what they make. If your salary increases $5,000, you spend an extra $2,000 on features for your car, you buy a new computer, a better couch, a bigger TV, and then you ask, "Where did all the money go?" Even though you needed none of the above, now you need one more thing: another increase in your salary. So back you go to the corporate casino for one more try at the salary roulette wheel. I have never once seen anyone save the increase they received in their salary.

In other words, don't stay at the job for safe salary increases over time. That will never get you where you want—freedom from financial worry. Only free time, imagination, creativity, and an ability to disappear will help you deliver value that nobody ever delivered before in the history of humankind.

Too Many People at Your Company Can Make Major Decisions That Could Ruin Your Life

I don't like it when one person can make or break me. A boss. A publisher. A TV producer. A buyer of my company. At any one point I've had to kiss ass to all of the above. I hate it. I will never do it again.

The way to avoid this is to diversify the things you are working on so no one person or customer or boss or client can make a decision that could make you rich or destroy you or crush or even fulfill your life's dreams. I understand it can't happen in a day. But you can start planning now to create your own destiny instead of allowing people who don't like you to control your destiny. When you do this count, make sure the number comes to over twenty. Then when you spin the wheel the odds are on your side that a winning number comes up.

Your Job Probably Isn't Satisfying Your Needs

I will define "needs" the way I always do, via the four legs of what I call the Daily Practice. Are your physical needs, your emotional needs, your mental needs, and your spiritual needs being satisfied? The only time I've had a job that met all of these needs was when I had to do little work so that I had time on the side to either write, or start a business, or have fun, or spend time with friends. There were plenty of other times when I was working too hard, dealing with people I didn't like, getting my creativity crushed over and over, and so on. When you are in those situations, you need to plot out your exit strategy.

Your hands are not made to type out memos. Or put paper through fax machines. Or hold a phone up while you talk to people you dislike. One hundred years from now your hands will rot like dust in your grave. You have to make wonderful use of those hands now. Kiss your hands so they can make magic.

Someone might argue, "Not everyone is entitled to have all of those needs satisfied at a job." That's true. But since we already know that the salary of a job won't make you happy, you can easily modify lifestyle and work to at least satisfy more of your needs. And the more you can fulfill these needs, the more you will create the conditions for true abundance to come into your life.

Your life is a house. Abundance is the roof. But the foundation and the plumbing need to be in there first or the roof will fall down and the house will be unlivable. You create the foundation by following the Daily Practice. I say this not because I am selling anything but because it worked for me every time my roof caved in. My house has been bombed, my home has been cold, and blistering winds gave me frostbite, but I managed to rebuild. And that is how I did it.

Your Retirement Plan Is for S**t

I don't care how much you set aside for your 401(k). It's over. The whole myth of savings is gone. Inflation will carve out the bulk of your 401(k). And in order to cash in on that retirement plan you have to live for a really long time doing stuff you don't like to do. And then suddenly you're eighty and you're living a reduced lifestyle in a cave and can barely keep warm at night.

The only retirement plan is to choose yourself—to start a business or a platform or a lifestyle that allows you to put big chunks of money away. Some people can say, "Well, I'm just not an entrepreneur."

This is not true. *Everyone* is an entrepreneur. The only skills you need to be an entrepreneur are an ability to fail, an ability to have ideas and to sell those ideas, the courage to execute on those ideas, and to be persistent so even as you fail you learn and move on to the next adventure.

Or be an entrepreneur at work—an "entre-ployee." Take control of whom you report to, what you do, and what you create. Don't just do what's listed in your job description. That's the old way. Go beyond that. Or start a business on the side. Deliver some value, any value, to somebody, to anybody, and watch that value compound into a career.

Your other choice is to stay at a job where the boss is trying to keep you down, will eventually replace you, will pay you only enough for you to survive, will rotate between compliments and insults so you stay like a fish caught on the bait as he reels you in. You and I have the same twenty-four hours each day. Is that how you will spend yours?

I can already hear the excuses, because I've heard them all before. "I'm too old," "I'm not creative," "I need the insurance," "I have to raise my kids."
I was at a party once when a stunningly beautiful woman came up to me and said, "James, how are you!?"

What? Who are you?

I said, "Hey! I'm doing well." But I had no idea who I was talking to. Why would this woman be talking to me? I was too ugly. It took me a few minutes of fake conversation to figure out who she was.

It turns out she was the frumpish-looking woman who had been fired six months earlier from the job we were at. She had cried as she packed up her cubicle. At the time she was out of shape, she looked about thirty years older than she was, and now her life was going to go from better to worse. Until . . . she realized that she was out of the zoo.

What are you doing now?" I asked her. "Oh, you know," she said. "Consulting." Some people say, "I can't just go out there and consult. What does that even mean?"

And to that I answer, "OK, I agree with you." Who am I to argue? If someone insists they need to be in prison even though the door is unlocked, then I am not going to argue. They are free to stay in prison.

"I can't just *quit*!" people say. "I have bills to pay." But it's okay to take some baby steps.

I get it. Nobody is saying quit *today.* Before a human being runs a marathon he or she learns to crawl, then take baby steps, then walk, then run. Then exercise every day and stay healthy. Then run a marathon. (I *might* know what I am even talking about, since I can't run more than two miles without collapsing in agony.) But I do know that if you make the list right now, every dream, you can start to take those steps. I want to be a best-selling author. I want to reduce my material needs. I want to have freedom from many of the worries that I have succumbed to all my life. I want to be healthy. I want to help all of the people around me or the people who come into my life. I want everything I do to be a source of help to people. I want to only be around people I love, people who love me. I want to have time for myself.

These are not goals. These are *themes.* What do I need to do to practice those themes every day? It starts the moment I wake up. I ask, "Who can I help today?" I ask the darkness when I open my eyes. "Who would you have me help today?" I'm a secret agent and I'm waiting for my mission. This is how you take baby steps. This is how eventually you run toward freedom.

⸺᠆⊙᠆⸺

ABUNDANCE WILL NEVER COME FROM YOUR JOB

Only stepping out of the prison imposed on you from your factory will allow you to achieve abundance. You can't see it now. It's hard to see the gardens when you are locked in jail. Abundance only comes when you are moving along your themes—when you are truly enhancing the lives of the people around you.

It happens when you wake up every day with that motive of enhancement. Enhance your family, your friends, your colleagues, your clients, potential customers, readers, people who you don't even know yet but you would like to know. Become a beacon of enhancement and then, when the night is gray, all of the boats will move toward you, bringing their bountiful riches.

BE AN IDEA MACHINE

The way to have good ideas is to get close to killing yourself. It's like weightlifting. When you lift slightly more than you can handle, you get stronger. Then you add more to that, and more to that, until the muscle keeps getting stronger. Your idea muscle works the same way. If you're broke and close to death, you have to start coming up with ideas. If you destroy your life, you need to come up with ideas to rebuild it.

The only time I've been *forced* to have good ideas is when I was up against the wall. My life insurance policy was like a gun to my head: "Come up with good ideas . . . or else your kids get your life insurance!" Or at an airport when I realized a business I had been working on for four years was worthless. Or when I was getting a divorce and I was lonely and afraid I wouldn't make any money again, or I wouldn't meet anyone again.

The problem is that we're *not* in a state of panic most of the time. States of panic are special and have to be revered. Think about the times in your life that you remember—it's exactly those moments when you hit bottom and were forced to come up with ideas, to get stronger, to connect with some inner force inside you with the outer force.

This is why it's important *now* to strengthen that connection to that idea force inside of you. This chapter is about *how*. Nothing you ever thought of before amounted to anything—that's why you are exactly where you are at that moment of hitting bottom. Because all of the billions of thoughts you've had led you to right there. You can't trust the old style of thinking anymore. You have to come up with a new way of thinking. A new way of having ideas. A new way of interacting with the outside universe.

You're in crisis. Time to change. Time to become an *Idea Machine*.

My life has changed 100 percent for the better every six months since I started following the Idea Machine practice. It's moved me to the upper right quadrant of the Idea Matrix (see the Introduction). It's flooded me with ideas. It's made me money. It's changed my life.

People know what a second wind is. It's when you are running for a long time, at the point of exhaustion. At that moment, something kicks in and gives you a second boost of energy. Four hundred thousand years ago people didn't jog for exercise. They didn't even have jogging shorts or sneakers. Four hundred thousand years ago people needed to eat and live. And either they were running to catch prey or they were running from a lion. In both cases they needed that second wind, or else, they died.

The same thing happens in the brain today that happened 400,000 years ago. When you are about to die, a second wind kicks in. Ideas, experiences, opportunity, and probably hidden forces and neurochemicals we don't understand. But you can't get a second wind unless you're *already* in good shape. It's not possible unless you are already able to run long distances. This is why it's important to exercise the idea muscle right now. If your idea muscle atrophies, then you won't have any ideas. How long does it take this muscle to atrophy? The same as any other muscle in your body: just two weeks without having any ideas. Just as, if you lie down in a bed for two weeks and don't move your legs, you will need physical therapy to walk again.

Many people need idea therapy. Not so that they can come up with great ideas right this second (although maybe you will) but so that they can come up with ideas when they need them: when their car is stuck, when their house blows up, when they are fired from their job, when their spouse betrays them, when they go bankrupt or lose a big customer, or lose a client, or go out of business, or get sick.

Ideas are the currency of life. Not money—because money can run out. Money gets depleted until you go broke. But good ideas buy you good experiences, buy you better ideas, buy you better experiences, buy you more time, save your life. Financial wealth is a side effect of the "runner's high" of your idea muscle. I've often written about the idea muscle as part of what I call my Daily Practice. Every day I have to check the box on physical, emotional, mental, and spiritual health.

And I get a lot of questions about it so I will try and answer them here. Sometimes people ask, "Did you only start coming up with ideas because you already had it made?"

Answer: I was on the floor crying because I was dead broke and dead lonely and had no prospects, so that's why I had to do it.

Here are some other questions I've gotten, in no particular order.

What do You Mean by an "Idea Machine?"

You will be like a superhero. It's almost a guaranteed membership in the Justice League of America. You will have a ton of ideas for every situation you are in. Any question you are asked, you will know the response. You will take every meeting you attend so far out of the box that you'll be on another planet. If you are stuck on a desert highway, you will figure the way out.

After I started exercising the idea muscle, it was like a magic power had been unleashed inside of me. It's OK if you don't believe me. There are many times when I don't have ideas. But that's when I stop practicing what I am about to advocate.

Try it for yourself. Its like a part of your brain has opened up and a constant flow of stuff, both good and bad, gets dropped in there. From where? I don't think about it and I don't care. Because I use it and it works for me.

The year 2009 was one of those times when I desperately needed to do this. I spent all of my time either trying to find a girlfriend or trying to start a business or both. I was also going broke in the stock market and losing my home.

Every night, I'd have waffles for dinner and a bottle of wine and start writing ideas down. This is before I went paleo (no waffles allowed!) and stopped drinking alcohol (five years sober!) and I was writing ten to twenty of the most ludicrous ideas a day down. And you know what? It worked.

How do I Start Exercising the Idea Muscle?

Take a waiter's pad. Go to a local café. Maybe read an inspirational book for ten to twenty minutes. Then start writing down ideas. What ideas? Hold on a second. The key here is, write ten ideas.

Why a Waiter's Pad?

A waiter's pad fits in your pocket so you can easily pull it out to jot things down. It's too small to write a whole novel or even a paragraph. In fact, it's specifically designed to help you make a list. And that's all you want, a list of ideas. A waiter's pad is a great conversation starter if you are in a meeting. Someone at the meeting will inevitably say, "I'll take fries with my burger," and everyone will laugh. You broke the ice and you stand out.

Waiter's pads are cheap. You can get about a hundred for ten dollars. This shows you are frugal and don't need those fancy moleskin pads to have a good idea.

Why Ten Ideas?

If I say, "write down ten ideas for books you can write," I bet you can easily write down four or five. I can write down four or five right now. But at six it starts to get hard. "Hmmm," you think, "what else can I come up with?" This is when the brain is sweating. It's like when you exercise in the gym and your muscles don't start to build until you break a sweat. Your metabolism doesn't improve when you run until you sweat. Your body doesn't break down the old and build the new until it is sweating. The poisons and toxins in your body don't leave until you sweat. The same thing happens with the idea muscle. Somewhere around idea number six, your brain starts to sweat. This means it's building up. Break through this. Come up with ten ideas.

———⟋∞⟍———

WHAT IF I JUST CAN'T COME UP WITH TEN IDEAS?

You are putting too much pressure on yourself. Perfectionism is the *enemy* of the idea muscle. Perfectionism is your brain trying to protect you from harm—from coming up with an idea that is embarrassing and stupid and could cause you to suffer pain.

You actually have to shut the brain off to come up with ideas. And the way to do this is by forcing it to come up with bad ideas. So let's say you've written five ideas for books and they are all pretty good. And now you are stuck. "How can I top this brilliant list of five?"

Well, let's come up with some bad ideas. Here's one: *Dorothy and the Wizard of Wall Street.* Dorothy is in a hurricane in Kansas and she lands right at the corner of Broadway and Wall Street in NYC and she has to make her way all the way down Wall Street in order to find "The Wizard of Wall Street" (Lloyd Blankfein, CEO of Goldman Sachs) in order to get home to Kansas. Instead, he offers her a job to be a high-frequency trader instead.

What a bad idea! OK, now go on to the next fifteen ideas. (And if anyone wants to buy the movie rights to *The Wizard of Wall Street*, please contact Claudia on Twitter @ClaudiaYoga.)

———⟋∞⟍———

HOW DO I KNOW IF AN IDEA IS A GOOD ONE?

You won't. You don't. You can't. You *shouldn't.* Let's say you come up with ten ideas a day. In a year you will come up with 3,650 ideas (no breaks on weekends, by the way, if you want to get good at this). It's unlikely that you came up with 3,650 good ideas (after you become an Idea Machine your ratio goes up, but probably in the beginning your ratio of bad ideas to good is around a thousand to one).

Don't put pressure on yourself to come up with good ideas. The key right now is just to have ideas, period. When Tiger Woods is practicing he doesn't get disappointed in himself if he doesn't hit a hole in one every shot. You're just practicing here. Practice doesn't make perfect. But practice makes permanent. So that later on when you do need good ideas to save your life, you know you will be a fountain of them. When there's a tidal wave of good ideas coming out of you, you only need a cup of water out of that to quench your thirst.

How Do I Execute My Ideas?

Here's what I do often when I am writing down ideas that I think I might want to act on: I divide my paper into two columns. In one column is the list of ideas. In the other column is the list of "First Steps"—*only* the first step, because you have no idea where that first step will take you. Imagine you are driving one hundred miles to your home late at night. You turn on your headlights so you can see in front of you. All you can see is about thirty feet in front of you but you know if you have the lights on the entire time, you'll make it home safely, one hundred miles away. Activating the Idea Machine is how you turn the lights on so you can get home. But you don't need to do any more than that.

Richard Branson, founder of the Virgin Atlantic Airlines, is an Idea Machine. And he provides one of my favorite examples of taking a critical first step. Branson didn't like the service on some airline he was flying. So he had an idea: "I'm going to start a new airline." But how the heck can a magazine publisher start an airline from scratch with no money?

No idea is so big you can't take the first step. If the first step seems too hard, make it simpler. And don't worry again if the idea is *bad*. This is all practice. So Branson's first step was to call Boeing to see if they had an airplane he could lease. (More on his next steps in a later chapter).

In 2006 I had ten ideas for websites I wanted to build. I knew how to program but didn't want to. So my first step was to find a site like Elance and then put the specs up and find programmers in India who could make the websites for me. I paid one of them $2,000 to develop a site I sold for $10 million nine months later. Nine of the ten ideas were bad. But you only need one good one.

If I'm Coming Up with Business Ideas, How Do I Know if I'm on The Right Track?

There's no way to know in advance if a business idea is a good one. Google started around 1996 but didn't make a dime of money until around 2001.

My favorite example is a software company called Odeo that helped people set up podcasts. Since I do a podcast now, this seems like a great idea to me. So they raised a ton of money from professional venture capitalists. Then one of their programmers started working on a side project. The side project got a little traction but not much.

But the CEO of Odeo decided to switch strategies and go full force into the side project without having a clue if it would work. He felt bad, since this wasn't what the investors had invested in. So he called up all of the investors and described the side project to them and all the traction they were getting, etc., and then made an offer: "Since this is a different direction, I'd be willing to buy all of your shares back so nobody will lose any money." One hundred percent of his investors said, *"Yes! Give it back!"* and so he bought all of his investors' shares back. The side project was Twitter—and now founder Ev Williams is a billionaire as a result. Nobody knew. Nobody knows. You have to try multiple ideas and see which ones create excitement among customers and employees, and you can see that people are legitimately using it and excited by it.

When I started Stockpickr, (what I called then "the MySpace of Finance") someone once wrote me and said, "Please block me from the site. I'm too addicted to it and it's ruining my life." That's when I had a sense that I had a halfway decent idea. And that was one of ten ideas I was trying simultaneously. The rest failed. So don't be afraid to test, fail, test, fail, try again, repeat, improve, test, fail again, and keep improving. The way to keep improving is to keep coming up with ideas for your business and for other new businesses.

As your idea muscle improves, so will your ability to "fail quickly"—which is a much more crucial skill to hone than executing quickly.

Speaking of Failing Quickly…When Do I Shut Down an Idea?

In 2009, I started The Leading Love Site on the Net. It was going to be a dating website where your Twitter feed was your profile. Everyone I spoke to said, "That's a great idea!" I had already raised money and was raising more. Then, on the day I was going to close the fund-raising round I woke up shaking. I had this vision of myself a year from now explaining to all of the investors why it wasn't going to work. So I returned all the money. I was out the money I had spent to create the website. I can guess why I realized it was a bad idea (people on dating sites want to be anonymous, for instance), but I didn't really know at the time. I just had that feeling that I had to return the money.

When your idea muscle is developed along with the other legs of the Daily Practice—physical, emotional, mental, and spiritual—you'll have a better idea when you should shut things down. And you'll know that you are shutting them down for the right reasons. At this point, you are "failing quickly" as opposed to self-sabotaging or fearing success or just being stupid.

How Do You Keep Track of Your Ideas?

I make a list of ideas and then I usually just throw it out. The whole purpose is to exercise the idea muscle. I know most of the ideas are bad ideas, so there's no sense keeping them around. If one of the ideas is good, then I will probably remember it and build on it for the next day. Sometimes it's kind of funny, when I come across an old list of ideas, to see what I was thinking. Every now and then I think I find a good idea in my old lists, but it's rare. And then what do I do with that rare good idea? Probably nothing.

Are All of Your Ideas Business Ideas?

No. It's hard to come up with over 3,000 business ideas a year. I'm lucky if I come up with a few business ideas. The key is to have fun with it. Or else you don't do it. People avoid things that are not fun.

Here are some of the types of lists I make:

- IDEA SEX. Combine two ideas to come up with a better idea. Don't forget that idea evolution works much faster than human evolution. You will *always* come up with better ideas after generations of idea sex. This is the DNA of all idea generation.
- OLD TO NEW. Ten old ideas I can make new. (Dorothy on Wall Street, etc). It's similar to idea sex, but with a twist.
- Ten ridiculous things I would invent (the smart toilet, etc).
- Ten books I can write (Ex: *The Choose Yourself Guide to an Alternative Education*, etc).
- Ten business ideas for Google/Amazon/Twitter.

- Ten people I can send ideas to.
- Ten podcast ideas I can do, or videos I can shoot ("Lunch with James," a video podcast where I just have lunch with people over Skype and we chat).
- Ten industries where I can remove the middleman.
- Ten ways to make old posts of mine and make books out of them.
- Ten ways I can surprise Claudia. (Actually, more like one hundredways. That's hard work!)
- Ten items I can put on my "ten list ideas I usually write" list.
- Ten people I want to be friends with and I figure out what the next steps are to contact them (Azaelia Banks, I'm coming after you! Larry Page better watch out also.)
- Ten things I learned yesterday.
- Ten things I can do differently today. Right down my entire routine from beginning to end as detailed as possible and change one thing and make it better.
- Ten chapters for my next book.
- Ten ways I can save time. For instance, don't watch TV, drink, have stupid business calls, don't play chess during the day, don't have dinner (I definitely will not starve), don't go into the city to meet one person at a time for coffee, don't waste time being angry at that person who did X, Y, and Z to you, and so on.
- Ten things I learned from X, where X is someone I've spoke to recently or read a book by recently. I've written posts on this about the Beatles, Mick Jagger, Steve Jobs, Bukowski, the Dalai Lama, Superman, *Freakonomics*, etc.
- Ten things women totally don't know about men. (that turned into a list of one hundred and Claudia said to me, "Uh, I don't think you should publish this").
- Today's list: Ten more alternatives to college I can add to the book I'm work-

ing on to be called *Forty Alternatives to College.*

- Ten things I'm interested in getting better at (and then ten ways I can get better at each one).

- Ten things I was interested in as a kid that might be fun to explore now. (Like, maybe I can write that "Son of Dr. Strange" comic I've always been planning. And now I need ten plot ideas).

- Ten ways I might try to solve a problem I have. This has saved me with the IRS countless times. Unfortunately, the Department of Motor Vehicles is impervious to my superpowers.

- This is just a sample. Every day, come up with ten ideas. The other day I thought of "ten ways I can release more endorphins into my body." Today, "ten ways I can help people build their Idea Machine." Tomorrow is "ten ways I can turn my next book into a webinar for Oprah."

<hr/>

Is The Idea Muscle The Most Important Part Of What You Call The Daily Practice?

No! They are all *equal*. Remember what I said about sitting on a stool with four legs. If someone pulls away one of the legs you might still balance and the stool stays up, but it's tricky. If someone pulls two legs off, you're down for the count.

The Daily Practice is to be physically, emotionally, mentally (the idea muscle), and spiritually healthy. If you aren't physically healthy you won't come up with ideas. You'll be coughing and vomiting.

If you are around people who hate you, you won't come up with ideas. Because they will be yelling at you while you are trying to think. And if you aren't feeling grateful and calm in your life on a regular basis, then you will be anxious and it will be harder to come up with ideas. So all four parts of the Daily Practice work together to come up with great ideas.

Do I Really Do This Every Day?

Let's say you get tired for a day of writing ideas. Then just try something different. The key is to keep activating parts of your brain that have atrophied. Sometimes if I don't feel like writing down a list of ten ideas I'll do something else—say, draw ten eyes. Or make a collage. Or take photographs of the ten most beautiful women I see today. Or the ten ugliest men (if I take picture of the ten most handsome men, then I might get jealous and that's a whole other thing I'd have to deal with). Or I might go make ten prank calls (well, when I was a kid I did that. I never do that now! Maybe).

Is It Important To Read Before Writing?

I don't know. But I do. At any given point I have about ten to twenty books on my "to go" list—books that I can just pop into and continue reading. Every day I read at least 10 percent of a nonfiction book that gives me tons of new ideas and similar portions of an inspirational book, a fiction book of high-quality writing, and maybe a book on games (lately I've been solving chess puzzles). And then I start writing.

Right now the inspirational book is *The Untethered Soul*. The nonfiction book is *Antifragile*. The fiction book is *Blind Date* (Kosinski), and the games book is actually my chess app (Shreder), which has nonstop puzzles. But this list changes almost every day.

How Long Does it Take Before I see Results?

It takes at least six months of coming up with ideas every day before you are an Idea Machine. Then your life will change every six months. I know I've said this before, but my life is completely different than it was six months ago, and six months before that, and so on. So different there is no way I could've predicted the differences. Six months ago I had no podcast. Now it's a big part of my day. Six months before that, *Choose Yourself!* had not come out. Six months before that, I had not yet accepted several board seats that have done well for me.

Do I Give My Ideas Away For Free?

When you come up with ideas for someone else, always give all the ideas away for free if you think they are good ideas (remember: six months). I read recently about one person who recommended giving *half* of your ideas away for free and making others pay for the other half. But this guarantees you will only come up with bad ideas, because you will hoard your ideas. You will develop a *scarcity complex* around your ideas.

Ideas are infinite. But once you define your capacity of good ideas (i.e., "half"), then they instantly become finite for you—not for anyone else.

If you operate according to an abundance mentality, and be grateful for the ideas that are flowing through you, then they will be infinite—and they will keep flowing. Where they come from, nobody knows.

So give ideas for free, and then when you meet others, give more ideas. And if someone wants to pay you and your gut feels this is a good fit, then give even more ideas.

I Keep Coming Up With Ideas That Keep Failing. What Do I Do?

here's this "cult of failure" that has popped up recently—this notion that you need to fail to succeed.

This is not necessarily true. Failure really sucks. You don't *want* to fail. But there is an easy way to solve this. Take the word *fail* out of your vocabulary.

Everything we do in life is a success. We breathe, we love, we practice kindness, and we deal with other human beings. We improve. We have experiences. This is magnificent and abundant success. Just even being able to try new things is something to celebrate every day. To smile at another person. To play. Most things I try to do don't work out as I planned. But who am I to predict the outcomes of my preparation? My only job is to prepare.

Everybody is a poor predictor of outcomes—from the weatherman, to the stock analyst. But we can all be good at preparation. And once I prepare, I show up at the starting line. Then the whistle blows, the race begins, I try my hardest with the most amount of integrity, and the results are not up to me. Then I go back and learn from the race, I prepare more, I love more, I celebrate more, and I show up for the next race. The whistle blows, and eventually good things happen. Preparation leads to faith in yourself.

Every moment, this moment while you are reading this, you get to choose abundance, gratitude, kindness, integrity, "goodness." Only you get to choose what is in your universe. When you don't choose, you excuse.

Is It Really Worth It To Become an Idea Machine?

I come up with ideas every day. I haven't had a business since 2009—and it failed, as mentioned above. Since then I've made more money than I know what to do with because I come up with ideas for people, for companies, for me, for people who have no idea who I am, for random anonymous things.

I then get invited to share my ideas. Sometimes I get paid for them. Sometimes I give them for free. Sometimes I get more introductions to people and sometimes I get a chance to advise companies that do well and make me money. And sometimes I write books. When you're an Idea Machine, everything you look at breaks down into a collection of ideas, just as physical objects would ultimately breakdown into collections of particles if your eyes were subatomic microscopes. Your eyes and brains become sub-idea microscopes that see the ideas that become the building blocks for everything in society. See them, build them, change them, seed them, birth them, love them, and live them. Ideas are the dark matter of the universe. We know it's there, but only those "in the know" can see them.

What Do I Do Once I Become an Idea Machine?

This is what I don't know the answer to because you are the master of your life. Now you're ready to take your unique place in the world. Now you have superpowers. You will know how to get to the Justice League satellite that orbits the Earth and solves problems at a moment's notice. You will know what to do. I don't know. Nobody else knows. You'll do it and the world won't be the same.

How to Sell Anything

Chances are, you are eventually going to want to try to sell one or some or all of your ideas.

I've never read a book on sales. They seemed corny to me. Like many other people, I always looked down on the concept of "selling." It seemed like something lower than me. To some extent, selling appears manipulative. You have a product, and you want to give potential buyers the perception that it has more value than it truly does. So you need to manipulate people to buy it. This seems sad, as in *Death of a Salesman* sort of sad. So I dismissed it. I was a sales snob.

But I was wrong. For the past twenty-five years all I have been doing is selling—products, services, businesses, and myself. Sometimes I have been manipulative. And sometimes I've sold things I've had such passion for cheap just because I wanted to get the message out about what I was selling. And often, it was very much in the middle: I needed to sell something because I had to pay my bills. Maybe I was a little desperate, a little hopeful, a little scared, and I wanted to make sure my family got fed.

Our basic needs cost money. And as we get older, we become responsible for others' basic needs. We become adults. Adults sell for today. Professionals sell for life.

These are the new rules of the economy—and all of this is from my own experience. That means they might not work for you, and that they might fly in the face of basic rules of salesmanship. I have no idea. But it's brought me such abundance, I can't *not* share it.

Over the past twenty-five years I've sold hundreds of millions of dollars of stuff. That stuff being everything in Pandora's box that I had to sell just to stay alive. When I think what's worked for me in the realm of sales, here's what I come up with:

BE A FRIEND

Nobody is going to buy from someone they hate. The buyer has to like you and want to be your friend. People pay for friendship.

This sounds sort of whorish and it is. The times when I've hated myself the most were the times when I've prostituted myself to make money (this isn't as sexual as it sounds but it might as well be).

One time when I was raising money for a particular venture, the buyer was going through a business catastrophe and was worried he would go out of business. I didn't like him but I called him every day for three months at the same time to see if he "wanted to talk" and to offer my advice on how he should deal with his situation. I eventually raised a lot of money from him even though the first time I met him he was honest with me and said, "It seems like you don't know your industry very well." Which just goes to show: friendship outweighs almost every other factor in selling.

Another time I wanted to do a website for ABC.com. The main decision maker was involved with a school in Harlem for charity. I went up there for four weeks in a row and played twenty kids simultaneously in chess. Everyone had fun. I got the website job. My competitors were all bigger, better financed, and probably better. But I was the one who spent time with the people who mattered to the person hiring. I was the one who showed that I cared.

Unfortunately, I didn't like either of those people personally. And eventually, I lost the business. The only good outcomes arise when both sides like each other. At one point I was so sick of my new "friendships" I went to see a therapist and uttered the clichéd line, "I don't even know who I am anymore because I hate all my friends and all my friends are customers so I'm their slave friend."

Now I only do business with people I like. The fastest way to lose all your money and mutilate your heart is to work with people you don't like. I will never do that again. And you don't have to do it either, despite what you might think.

Learn to Say No

When someone wants to do a big deal with you, it may be hard to say no. But no is valuable for several reasons:

Opportunity cost. Instead of pursuing something you really don't want to do, you could free up time and energy to find something more lucrative or something you would enjoy more. Opportunity cost is the one *biggest* cost in all of our lives. We spend it like there's no tomorrow.

And guess what? Eventually there's no tomorrow.

Supply and demand. If you reduce the supply of you by saying no, then the demand for you goes up and you make more money—and have more fun.

You'll hate yourself. I see this every day, particularly in my own life. The reason I can write about this is not because I'm an expert. We don't write about the things we *know*. We write about the things that are deep down *challenges* for us right now. When I say yes to something I don't want to do, I end up hating myself, hating the person I said yes to, doing a bad job, and disappointing everyone. I try try try not to do it anymore.

Over-deliver

If someone pays a hundred dollars and you give them just a hundred dollars in value, then you just failed. F.A.I.L.E.D. You'll never sell to that person again. That's fine in some situations, but in most situations it's no good. If someone pays a hundred dollars you need to give them $110 in value.

Think of that extra ten dollars as going into some sort of karmic bank account that pays interest (as opposed to a US bank account). That money grows and compounds. Eventually, there's real wealth there. And that wealth translates into wealth in the real world. Most people are three-year-olds. They like to get presents.

People want to do business with people who give them presents. Over-delivering is a present. And it makes you feel good. Give and you will receive.

NEVER TAKE NO FOR AN ANSWER

This statement, which you've probably heard before, is usually applied incorrectly.

People think it means that you should keep pushing and trying new things until you get a yes. That's not what it means. Remember the first point above: be a friend, however flimsy that connection of friendship is. Follow them on Twitter, on Facebook. Say nice things about the person to other people. Never gossip.

Practice the art of the check-in. Send updates after the "no" on how the person is doing, how the product or service or business or whatever is doing. You don't need to check in every day. Maybe once a month. Maybe once a year. Who knows? Eventually you will find the yes with that person. It could be, and often is, up to twenty years later. You plant a seed and eventually the garden blooms.

UNDERPRICE

I once wanted to do the website for Fine Line Films. I loved their movies. I met the guy running their site. He kept saying over and over again, "We can't afford a lot," and I kept saying, "Don't worry about it" and would show him more and more of our work. Eventually we did the websites for every one of their movies And got paid $1,000 per website. Then, when Con Edison wanted to hire us, Nevin at Fine Line was a reference.

I write for a lot of places right now for free. Any medium I love, I am willing to write for. It's like a dream come true for me. The benefits from doing that have been incalculable. Not always financial, but always real.

We are a combination of many constituencies inside of our bodies and minds. Financial is just one. But all of our constituencies need to work together to make us well balanced and peaceful.

The art of selling, for me, is to have everything inside of me working together.

Be The Source

One time I wanted to buy a company. The details of how I would do that are sort of obscure and not important. The company is well-known in the financial media space. At the critical moment, the owner called me and said, "What should I do? I have this other offer and I have your offer." He described the other offer to me. I told him to take it.

I missed out on what could've been a lot of money to me. But there was a slight chance we would've all gone bust. Now the buyer is thriving, and eight years later he is a friend. Will we ever do business together? I can't predict the future. But I know I delivered value to another human being. That value is real and I can put it to use whenever I want.

Often the best way to make friends and customers for life is to direct them to a better service or product than yours. Be the source of valuable information rather than the source of your "product of the day." Of course, this is different from the old way, when the goal was just to sell your product and do what was best for you, rather than to help your customer get what was best for them. But in the human economy, they won't just think of you as someone who sells to them. They will know forever that you are a trusted source. Trust is worth more than next month's rent being paid. Trust builds a bridge that will never wear out. At some point in the distant future, when you are on the run in every other way, you may need to cross that bridge.

SELL EVERYTHING

What you offer is not just your product. Your offering is product, services, your employees, your experiences, your ideas, your other customers, and even (as mentioned above) your competitors. So sell them all. When you are good at what you do, the product or service you offer is just the way people build the first link to you. It's the top of a huge pyramid.

But the base of the pyramid, the real service, is when customers have access to you and you can provide advice and the full power of your network and experience. This is when you are over-delivering on steroids and how you build real wealth—not just a one-time fee for a service or product.

Many people say, "No! My product is high margin and I want to make money when I sleep."

In the long run, nobody cares about your product. In the long run, it is the entire holistic view of your offering, your service, you, that you are selling. Without that, you will build a mediocre business that may or may not pay the bills. With that, you will create wealth.

SELL THE DREAM

People can see what your product is right now. What they want to know is . . . the future. Will your product make them more money? Will it get them a promotion? Maybe even, will *you* hire them if they buy your product?

When you get in the door, do not sell your product. People make a decision on your product in five seconds. Sell the dream. Build up images of the dream. Give a taste of what the dream is like. Let it linger. Let it weave itself. Let the imagination of the buyer take hold and run with it. The dream has up to infinity in value.

But then, you might ask, do I risk under-delivering?

Answer: Yes. Don't do that. Be as good as the dream.

FIRE CUSTOMERS

This is similar to "Saying No," with the one difference that you have already made a sale. And if it's not going well or if it's leaving a bad taste somewhere inside of you—or if the customer has gone from friend to enemy for whatever reason and it seems like there is no repair—then fire your customer. The sooner the better.

This applies not just to customers but everyone in your life. *Everyone.*

If someone no longer has your best interest at heart, then in your own self-interest you need to back off. Now. A bad customer (a bad person) spreads like a disease inside you, your employees, your other customers, your competitors, your future customers, your family, etc.

"But what if it's my biggest customer? How do I pay the bills?"

I don't know. Figure it out. You have to or you will die.

When I tell people to build their "idea muscle" (by writing down ten ideas, good or bad, every day) it's not so they can come up with great business ideas (although they might). It's so they can come up with ideas *in situations like this.* This is where being an Idea Machine saves your life and saves everything around you. But remember: bad customers will kill you and your family and your friends.

PERSUASION

Your best new customers are your old customers. If you need to make more money or build a new business, then go to your customers (who are now your friends) and tell them, "I need advice. What other service can I provide you or anyone you know?"

It might be something totally unrelated to your business. It doesn't matter. Do it. It might be that your customer is looking for a new job. That's great. Make it your business to find him a new job. Now you have a new customer.

It might be your customer needs a boyfriend. OK, introduce her to all of your friends who might be good for her. If you've been following this approach to sales, then your customers are now your friends, are now your family, are now the lifeblood of how you wake up in the morning.

We spend years building a garden. We plant the seeds. We tend the soil. We water the plants. But we are also the sun. The sun shines no matter what. It doesn't care which flower blossoms. The sun is always there providing value every second of the day. Be the sun and you will create abundance.

I don't know the buzzwords to make a sale. I'm not very good at shaking hands. I don't take people out to baseball games or do any of the things I see other people do. But I've been selling for twenty-five years. And whenever I've been dead broke, depressed, and suicidal, I've picked myself up and sold again and again.

I'm a salesman. And I'm proud of it.

How to Convince Anyone of Anything in Sixty Seconds

Selling will require you to have a lot of conversations and attempt to convince a lot people of various things. Think of it this way: you're on the most important elevator ride of your life. You have ten seconds to pitch—the classic "elevator speech." Love or hate. Money or despair. And you may never get this chance again.

I've been on both sides of this equation. I've had people pitching me. But mostly, I've been scared and desperate and afraid to ask someone to give me, want me, love me, all in the time of an elevator ride. Perhaps the hardest thing for me was when I was doing my "3am" Web series for HBO. I had to walk up to random strangers at three in the morning on the streets of New York City and convince them within five seconds to spill their most intimate secrets to me rather than kill me. Not quite an elevator pitch but the same basic idea. I had a lot of practice. I probably approached over 3,000 people cold. In some cases people tried to kill me. In one case I was chased. In other cases people opened up their hearts, and I am infinitely grateful to them.

The ideas below have worked for me in the hundreds of times I've had to be persuasive—either in writing, or in person, in business, or in friendships and in love. I hope variations on it can work for you. You decide.

Let People Know Who You Are

People want to know they are talking to a good, honest, reliable person that they can trust and perhaps even like, or love. Yes, love.

They won't love you by looking at your résumé. You have to do some method acting. Before you even you're your mouth, imagine what your body would feel like if your customer has already said yes. You would be standing up straight, smiling, palms open, ready to close the deal. You have to method act at the beginning of your pitch. If you are slouched and your head is sticking out, then your brain is not as well connected to your nervous system and you won't be in the "flow."

I can drag out the science here, but this is a chapter in a book, not a peer-reviewed scientific paper. The reality is, when you're slouched over, not only are you not using the full potential of your brain, but you don't look confident, or even trustworthy. And who wants to do business with you then?

Relax and Breathe

Think about how you breathe when you are anxious and nervous. I will tell you how I breathe: short, shallow breaths in the upper chest. So do the reverse before a ten-second pitch.

Breathe deep and in your stomach. Even three deep breaths in the stomach (and when you inhale, try to imagine your stomach almost hitting your back) have been shown to totally relax the mind and body. People sense this. Again, this builds trust and relaxes you.

Now, even though you haven't said a single word, you've probably done the two most important things for persuading someone.

Lose The "Uhhh. Yeah. Uhhh. Mmm-Hmm. Uh-huh's"

I have a hard time with this. It seems natural to say, "yup" or "right" or "uh-huh" or whatever. But here are the facts (and, again, there have been studies on this): people perceive you as stupid when you do this. Just keep quiet when someone is talking.

Then, when they're done speaking, wait for two seconds before responding. They might not be done yet. And it gives you time to think of a response. If you are thinking of a response while they are talking, then you aren't listening to them. People unconsciously know when you are not listening to them. Then they say no to you.

Remember The Four U's

Finally, now we're getting to the heart of the matter. *The actual nuts and bolts of persuasion.*

I've googled "the 4 U's" and each time I get a different set of four. So I'm going to use the four that have worked for me the best.

This is not BS, or a sneaky way to convince someone to do something they don't want to do. This is a way for you to consolidate your vision into a sentence or two and then express it in a clear manner. This is the way to bond and connect with another person's needs instead of just your own pathetic wants. You can use this in an elevator pitch, on a date, with your children, on your mother—whatever. But it works. Think about these things when talking.

Urgency

Why the problem you solve is *urgent* to your demographic. For example: "I can never get a cab when it rains!" So what's the solution here? How does your offering address this urgency?

Unique

Why is your solution unique? "We aggregate hundreds of car services into one simple app. Nobody else does this."

Useful

Why is your solution useful to the lives of the people you plan on selling to or deliver your message to? "We get you there on time."

Ultra-specific

This shows there is no fluff. "Our app knows where you are. Your credit card is preloaded. You hit a button and a car shows up in four to five minutes." Of course the example I give is for Uber, but you can throw in any other example you want. I'll throw in a fifth U.

User-friendly

Make it as easy as possible for someone to say yes. Give them a money-back guarantee, for instance, or a giveaway. Or higher equity. Or testimonials from people you both know. Etc.

Oh! And before I forget, a sixth U:

Unquestionable Proof

You can show this in the form of profits, or some measurable statistic. Or testimonials. Or a good wingman. Whatever it takes.

Have and Show Desire

A lot of people say you have to satisfy the desires of the other person in order for them to say yes. As much as we would like to think otherwise, people primarily act out of self-interest. The less they know you, the more they will do so. Otherwise they could potentially put themselves in danger.

We all know that kids shouldn't take candy from strangers. In an elevator pitch, the investor is the kid. What you are asking is the candy, and you are the stranger. So, unless you make the candy supersweet, their gut reflex is to say no. So make sure you make your candy sweeter by sprinkling in their desires. And what are their desires?

- Recognition
- Rejuvenation
- Relaxation
- Relief
- Religion
- Remuneration
- Results
- Revenge
- Romance

If you can help them solve these urgent problems or desires, then they are more likely to say yes to you.

I don't know what you are selling, but hopefully it's not to satisfy their desire for revenge. But if it is, don't do anything violent.

LEARN HOW TO HANDLE OBJECTIONS

Everyone is going to have gut objections. They've been approached thousands of times before. Do you know how many times I've been approached to have sex in an elevator?

None.

But probably many others have and you have to put up with nonstop objection. I will list them and then give solutions in parentheses:

- NO TIME.

  (That's OK. It's on an elevator. So they have elevator-length time. The key here is to stand straight and act like someone who deserves to be listened to).

- NO INTEREST.

  (You solve this by accurately expressing the urgency of the problem.)

- NO PERCEIVED DIFFERENCE between what you offer and what's already out there.

  (But you have your unique difference ready to go.)

- NO BELIEF.

  (Offer unquestionable proof that this works.)

- NO DECISION.

  (Make their decision as user-friendly as possible.)

With great power comes great responsibility. Most people don't have the power of persuasion. They mess up on each of the points I've outlined above. It takes practice and hard work.

But this is not just about persuasion. It's not about money. It's not about the idea. It's not about yes or no. It's about connection.

It's about two people, who are probably strangers, reaching through physical and mental space and trying to understand each other and reach common ground. It's not about money. It's not about the idea. It's not about yes or no. It's about two people falling in love.

ONCE THE IDEAS GET ROLLING...: TEN THINGS YOU NEED TO KNOW ABOUT LEADING

They fired me. They fired me as CEO. Then they fired me as a board member. Then they took away my shares. And now none of them ever talk to me. I started the company, I had the initial idea, I raised $30 million for it from A-plus investors (i.e., "rich people"). I bought two companies for it, I hired the first fifty employees, and then I was shown the door.

The reason? I was a bad leader. Here are some things I didn't know about my own company: I didn't know what our product did. I didn't know any of the clients. I didn't know how much money we made. I didn't know how much we lost. And I had crushes on the secretaries and maybe two or ten other employees. I would've gladly stuck my tongue in the ears of any of those employees. Ewwww! But why was I fired? I just didn't *do* anything... for... anyone. I never wanted to talk. I would lock myself in my office and people would knock and I would pretend not to be there. If anyone wanted to talk to me about "vision" I would just nod my head and say something like, "make it happen," like I was Captain Picard on the Starship *Enterprise.*

Being a leader doesn't mean you are the guy who runs things. Being a leader doesn't mean you created something or you did something great in the past or some other person has given you any kind of authority. Being a leader happens *right now,* today. It's something you can do without money, without authority, and without anybody. But first, you have to lead yourself. It's a mind-set. I'm going to make a list (surprise!). Feel free to add to the list or include your own experiences.

In fact, I would really appreciate if you did.

After running twenty or so companies (most of them failures), after investing in thirty companies (most of them successes), after advising or being on the board of a dozen companies (most of them successes), and after being married twice (50 percent success rate), I have a sense of what I think a leader is today. It has changed vastly from what it used to be. The skills are different, but the underlying idea is the same.

Desire More Success for Others Than for Yourself

Most important by far is that you be able to care about others' success more than your own. Everyone around you needs to ultimately become better than you. That's how you lead. The light is in front of you and you take them to the light and then go back.

If all the people around you achieve more than you, then life will be good. I've seen this happen repeatedly. It doesn't matter if they are employees, investors, friends, or spouses. If you just focus on this one principle in all of your actions, then you are a leader. Today, figure out how the people around you can have a successful day.

Say "Yes, and..."

I just wrote a book called *The Power of No*. Buy it because your life will be better (and I am not ashamed of plugging it).

But now I'm about to tell you to say yes.

Claudia had an idea for a joke this morning that she wants to start a talk off with. I had a suggestion to change it. I didn't say, "Don't do that. Do this." I said, "Yes, and . . ." a technique used in improvisational comedy. What does it mean? I trust Claudia and value her thoughts, so I if I just say no it shows I haven't been respectful enough of the time she put into coming up with an idea.

So I say, "Yes, and . . ." then elaborate on what is good about her idea and how I think it can be made even better and why. I give all of her ideas and thoughts respect and add to them rather than ever subtract from them.

Constructive criticism works like this:

- You say, "Yes, and . . ."
- List what's good about the person's idea.
- Describe how you would improve it even more.
- Figure out the vision that is the base of the idea that you are talking about. Connect the "why" of what you are suggesting to the initial vision. Does it work better than the initial idea?
- Always be open to the fact that you might be wrong.

SHOW GRATITUDE

Yesterday I was talking to Lewis Howes, an athlete turned multimillion-dollar webinar and LinkedIn expert who was on my podcast a few months ago. Lewis told me that his outgoing voice mail says, "Before you leave me a message, tell me one thing you are grateful for." He says the messages people leave blow him away.

I always imagine a good leader is surrounded by people who call their mothers at the end of the day and tell them, "Mom, you can't believe what I did today. Let me tell you about it." Not that every day is fun. Because some work isn't. But your goal should be to make sure your employees can call Lewis Howes every day and have at least one new thing they can be grateful for.

Maybe they learned a new skill. Maybe they met a new client and created value for that client. Maybe a client they hated was fired. Because you can't let your employees get the disease that bad clients are all too happy to spread.

Follow The "30-150" Rule (AKA The Vision Rule)

An organization with less than thirty people is a tribe. There is evidence from 70,000 years ago that if a tribe got bigger than thirty people, it would split into two tribes.

A tribe is like a family—that is, you learn personally whom to trust and not to trust. You learn to care for their individual problems. You know everything about the people in your tribe. Having just thirty people in the tribe allows a leader to spend time with each person in the tribe and to listen to their issues.

When your organization grows from thirty to 150 people, you might not know everyone. But you know of everyone. You know you can trust Jill because Jack tells you you can trust Jill and you trust Jack.

Once that number gets past 150 people, it's impossible to keep track of everyone. But this is where humans split off from every other species. We united with one other by telling stories. We told stories of nationalism, religion, sports, money, products, better, great, *best!* If two people believe in the same story, they might be thousands of miles apart and total strangers—but they still have a sense they can trust each other.

And that is how a leader connects to all those people in his tribe, even the ones he or she doesn't know personally. *A leader tells a visionary story.* We are delivering the best service because… We are helping people in unique ways because… We have the best designs because… We treat people better because…

A good story starts with a problem, goes through the painful process of solving the problem, and has a solution that is better than anything ever seen before.

First you listened to people, then you took care of people, but now you unite people under a vision *they* believe in and trust and bond with.

Companies live and die by this. One company I advise grew themselves by buying two hundred regional offices, and then unifying them under one brand. The key to their success is how powerful the story will be that they tell of that brand. Why are they delivering the greatest value? People need to believe in the story.

———◯◯◯———

BE OK WITH CHANGE

Everyone has pain they don't want to feel. For instance, I might feel pain if someone makes fun of my looks. I used to feel pain if someone questioned my net worth, which I equated with self-worth. If I'm a CEO, I might have pain if the "numbers" go down.

So we do things to hide the pain. Imagine all the things we do as buffers for pain. We might wear nice clothes not because we like the clothes but because they are buffers for the pain: nobody will make fun of my looks. We might avoid going to the store because we don't want to run into the people who cause us pain. We might hide some numbers because we don't want investors to think we are bad CEOs. Soon, everything in our lives we might think gives us pleasure (because we are now avoiding all the pain) is actually just a buffer against pain and change. When you can get rid of the buffers against pain and change. life becomes more insecure, but you become free.

Luckily for you and for me, we live in a bigger world, a world where risk and beauty go hand in hand and we are no longer afraid of the underlying pains. A leader is always prepared for change, and realizes that pain is just an opportunity to live in a bigger and more abundant world. This is the secret that most people forget when they build their brick houses and hide inside from the outside world so pain doesn't seek them out.

———◯◯◯———

Know The Importance of Dignity

The other day someone canceled an appearance on my podcast at the last minute. I had rescheduled other meetings and even changed the time I would see one of my daughter's plays so I could interview this very successful entrepreneur. Now she wanted to reschedule again but I said no, even to the detriment of my podcast and all the people who work with me on the podcast who were looking forward to the interview. I wasn't angry with the person. She's running a business and was probably very busy. And people reschedule all the time. I just didn't like that it was last minute. I had studio time booked and no program to fill it.

I have a vision for my podcast. Everyone who comes on it is someone who has transformed their life and created the life they wanted. I want my guests' stories to help my listeners. The world is changing very fast and it's scary. I want to help people be less scared, and I know I am less scared when I hear the stories of my guests and learn from them. Although I'm relatively new at podcasting—I've only been doing it for 12 months —I treat my podcast as if it's already achieved the dream I have for it. It is a place where experts appear to help others deal with the crazy changes happening in our world and economy.

If I don't treat my own projects with respect, then how can I expect others to? If I don't treat myself with dignity, then how can I expect the people around me to treat me, or even one another, with dignity?

Know There's Always a Good Reason and a Real Reason for Everything, and Share It

When you are a leader, people come to you with problems every day. The problems are usually very good problems. "The client is asking for too much." Or "Jill didn't do her job right," or "My car broke down."

One time an employee asked to meet me outside the office. She was crying. I asked her what was wrong. She was afraid she was doing a bad job with a client. And she was. But it turned out the real problem was she had heard one of my business partners talking poorly about her behind her back and this was affecting her every day at work. This was what we truly needed to fix. And so we did. And then everything, employee, client, partner, etc., went well. One hundred percent of the time there is a good reason and a real reason for everything.

A leader listens to the good reason closely to try and figure out what the real reason is, and then comes up with a solution. And there is *always* a real reason. Listen for that and see if you can help. A good solution solves one problem. A real solution solves a hundred problems.

CARE ABOUT YOUR HEALTH

A sick leader is not a great leader. A leader who is spending time with people not good for them is not a good leader. A leader who doesn't constantly practice creativity is not a good leader. A leader who is not grateful for the abundance already in his or her life will never lead his vision into abundance. He won't know how.

There's no such thing as instant health. There's only such thing as practice and progress. All you have to do is check the box on progress. Progress compounds every day into enormous abundance.

LOVE WHAT YOU DO

Warren Buffett says he skips to work and that he would do the work he does for free. Maybe it's easy for him to say that because he has $50 billion. I've gone through and read his letters from the 1950s when he was first starting out. These letters are not publicly available. I had to really try hard to find them when I wrote my book on them in 2004.

Even back then, when he was broke and starting his business in his living room, you can tell by reading his letters that he loved what he did. He took glee in finding companies that nobody else knew about so nobody was looking when they became horribly undervalued, and he would then buy those companies.

Don't do something just for the money. Money is a side effect of persistence. You persist in things you are interested in. Explore your interests. Then persist. Then enjoy all the side effects.

Know How To Lead Yourself

You don't need to be leading anyone. Before I can lead anyone I have to lead myself. I have to read. I have to try and improve one percent a week. I have a handful of interests and I have a lot of experience. I have to get better at the things I'm interested in. I have to understand more deeply the painful experiences I've had. I have to every day practice the health—physical, emotional, mental, spiritual—that I suggest to everyone else. Sometimes I don't. And I feel it. But that's OK. Don't regret. Today is a new day. Today is the only day.

The definition of "success" for me is: "Is *today* successful?"

Because who knows if tomorrow will even exist? Today is the only day I need to think about success. And every successful tomorrow is determined by one thing: having a successful today.

SHARING IDEAS: BEING A GREAT PUBLIC SPEAKER

In order to do all the things discussed in the last chapter, leaders need to communicate with people. This often involves speaking to large groups at a time. There are polls that say that people would rather be dead than speak in public. Comedian Jerry Seinfeld joked that a guy giving a eulogy would rather be in the coffin.

I've given hundreds of talks, but for some reason, last week I wanted to die before I went on stage. I was speaking to an audience of about two hundred CEOs. I felt inadequate and that they would hate me. Claudia said, "Just take a deep breath. Do what you usually do." And I did. And I was fine.

Here's the operating theory: you don't need to spend 10,000 hours at anything to be the best. You just need to be pretty good at something (spend a couple of hundred hours) and then you need to know how to give a good talk in public. You will stand out, because so few people want to talk in public.

I wrote a post a while ago called "Tips to Be a Great Public Speaker." I still follow those tips, but since the first post I've given a lot more talks to a varied set of audiences. I've spoken about everything from spirituality to business to creativity to entrepreneurship to failure. And before each talk I've always thought to myself, "Holy s**t. How did I write that post about public speaking? I'm more nervous than ever!" So I've come up with a few more tips. And these tips for public speaking are as important as the ten I provided on leading in the previous chapter.

WATCH COMEDIANS

I watch great stand-up comedy before every talk. It puts me in a looser mood and makes me laugh, which relaxes me.

When possible, I will directly steal a joke from whatever comedian I'm watching. After all, they've tested out the joke, so it's probably a good one that will work for me as well. I even practice imitating their timing: the way they pause, the way they change voices and move around the stage, everything.

Comedians are the best public speakers and are up against the most brutal audiences, so you *must* study them. Learn from them.

DO NOT USE POWERPOINT

I used to think I always needed a PowerPoint presentation. Because as useful as my words are, we've all heard that a "picture is worth a thousand words." This is total BS. If a picture is worth a thousand words, then you are worth 100,000 pictures.

I compare comedian Daniel Tosh's stand-up with his TV show *Tosh.0*. His stand-up just involves him, making jokes—*no* PowerPoint, no visuals, no pictures worth a thousand words. The *Tosh.0* format involves him watching YouTube videos and making fun of them. His stand-up is better than the show. Even though the show is great, it isn't as fun as just watching him do stand-up. In a similar fashion, PowerPoint will only distract from the main attraction: *you.*

WEAR COMFORTABLE CLOTHES

I *only* dress in clothes I feel most comfortable in, even if everyone else is wearing tuxedos.

I wear a specific "uniform" when I speak: I wear a T-shirt I had custom made that has all 67,000 words of my book *Choose Yourself!* printed on it. And I wear a white shirt over it and black pants. Like a waiter. I'm at your service and I've chosen myself. BAM!

REMEMBER TO PAUSE

I had this unnatural fear that if I paused too much during a talk people would get bored.

But inserting pauses allows people to think about what you are saying. It allows you to breathe, to be funnier, and diminishes the impression that you are rushing through the material. Take a drink of water. Walk from one side of the stage to the other. Do whatever you need to do.

HAVE A Q&A PORTION

I enjoy Q&A as much as the talk itself. So I arrange beforehand to do the maximum amount of Q&A. Always good to have the audience as involved in your talk as you are.

ABS—*Always Be Storytelling. Never* give advice in a talk. Nobody, I don't care who you are, is smart enough to just dole out advice. Just talk about your own experiences and what you did to help yourself. Mix in interesting facts. Straight out advice will never help anyone. Buddha himself realized this about public speaking. He said, "Don't believe me on anything. Try this out for yourself."

ABV—*Always Be Vulnerable.* Nobody wants to hear from Invulnerable Man or Ms. Perfect. They want to hear where you are scared and vulnerable and feeling insecure, because we all are.

Poor speakers create an artificial divide between themselves and the audience. They feel they need to do this in order to establish their own credibility. Let me tell you—there is no such thing as credibility. In one hundred years there will be no buildings named after any of us. Somebody has to be on stage and some people have to be in the audience. That's the only difference.

Don't put any thought as to *why* you are on the stage or how you need to be "better" than the people in the audience. You aren't *better.* You're simply the speaker. We all woke up lonely and confused this morning. What a miracle that we get to speak to one another.

And even better, we feed the soul by listening to one another. Ultimately, the best speakers are the ones who have put 10,000 hours into listening.

DISCUSSING IDEAS: HOW TO NEGOTIATE WITH ANYONE

Every day for the past twenty years I've learned something new about negotiation. Communication is the thread that weaves humans into humanity. Make sure the result brings you life and love. Tomorrow is 100 percent based on the negotiations you do today. Constantly study yourself, the negotiations you've done, and try to improve so you don't experience the terrible effects of bad negotiations.

When I do what I tell you to do below—when I live life as gently and positively as possible—then my negotiations work out, and then my tomorrows and the tomorrows of the people around me are pleasant.

I've learned about negotiation while selling a company, buying a company, closing a sale, buying services, getting married, getting divorced, figuring out what to do with my life, screwing up my life (in a *big* way), and all the variety of things in life that happen in between. I haven't read any books on negotiation, and there may be better suggestions than what I've got for you. This is what works for me and I think what will work for others—but you have to try for yourself to find out for sure. Negotiate something today involving all of these things and tell me if they work.

SAY NO

I told this to someone the other day who is about to get fired from his job: don't *act* like it's a done deal. Getting fired is a legal action. It's always a negotiation with many more moving parts than people realize. Say no and that you need to "think about it." Your employer might well say something like, "This is not a negotiation." You can say, "That's OK. I need to think about this."

Give it twenty-four hours. Think about everything that's happened to you on the job. Think about what you need to get a new job or career. Employ the techniques listed below. In general, with everything you negotiate; give yourself permission to think about it. Or else it's manipulation and not negotiation.

DON'T BE A CHILD

Don't "meet in the middle." Here is a dumb negotiation scenario that never actually plays out in real life: You offer forty dollars, I offer twenty, and we meet in the middle at thirty.

The middle stuff never happens. Many people think it does so they always start off negotiations with being inauthentic. Always be honest. Say what you want and why. Negotiation equals authenticity. Without authenticity you lose the tires on your car. Then you end up going nowhere.

LET THE OTHER SIDE HELP YOU

There's the trick "I have to talk to X," where X is someone else you need to confirm your decision. But this is just a trick—one that works when you have it, and when you don't have it, it's useless. So I will give you a better trick: *get the other side of your negotiation to be* X. In other words, get them to negotiate against themselves.

The word *against* is probably the wrong word to use here. The only way the negotiation is going to work is if they are happy also. So "against" also means "for." They clearly want something from you. That's why you guys are at the table in the first place.

So here's how what you say: "I'm new at this. You guys are the grand masters of negotiation. If a grand master plays a novice, then he will always win. So help me out. What would you do if you were me?" And then *no matter what they say, you say,* "But seriously, if you were *me,* what would you do. Again, I'm just a novice. I have no clue what I'm doing. Help me out here." And they will help you out. Because they want the deal to close and you really do need their help, or else the deal will never close.

This isn't being inauthentic, because you want as much information on the table as possible. If they help you, then you have more information, and can be even more authentic. If anything, you might end up helping them more than they help you.

⸺∽⸺

Make Sure Your List is Bigger Than Theirs

Let's say you are negotiating a book advance. They offer a $10,000 advance and they can't budge higher. That's fine. Now make your list of other things: how much social media marketing will they do? What bookstores will they get you into? Who has control over book design? What percentage of foreign rights, of digital rights, can you get? Do royalties go up after a certain number of copies are sold? Will they pay for better book placement in key stores? Will they hire a publicist? And so on.

Make a list before every negotiation. Make the list as long as possible. If your list is bigger than theirs (size matters), then you can give up "the nickels for the dimes." This is not just about negotiation. This is to make sure that later you are not disappointed because there is something you forgot. Always prepare. Then you can have faith that because you prepared well, the outcome will also go well.

⸺∽⸺

KNOW YOUR SECRET VALUE

Let's say someone is buying your company. It may seem like all they are doing is buying the assets of your company. But they are also buying your company's "negative imprint." In other words, they are buying the fact that nobody else can buy your company." They can say, "Well, we don't care about that." Then fine. See if it's true. Offer your services to other companies. If you can't walk away from a negotiation, then you aren't negotiating. You're just working out the terms of your slavery.

IF IT'S NOT EASY, THEN WALK AWAY

If a negotiation is not easy, then it means you need to work harder to develop more value to offer. Negotiation should always be easy. If it's not, you need to take a step back and be patient for the moment when it becomes easy.

Never waste time chasing down a difficult negotiation. You will lose, you will be unhappy, the other side will be unhappy (even though they got you cheap, they will secretly think you are worthless), and you will have wasted time and squandered money.

IMPORTANT: Every day, your body requires energy to survive, to think, to do well, to be happy. You don't get infinite energy. One way to replenish energy is to sleep. The other way is to eat well and to exercise. But another way to replenish energy is to live a gentle life. As gently as possible. So your energy grows and is used where it is needed. Which means all negotiations need to be smooth else they result in anxiety and fear and guessing and out guessing and much future depletion of energy. And then you die faster than the one who lived gently.

Try this. Next time you are in a negotiation, don't forget to relax your face.

REALIZE THAT OPTIONS EQUAL FREEDOM

For instance, a freelance employee has the ability to take on more than one job. An employee can't take on more than one job, and everything he does on company time is owned by the company. That's slavery.

Let's say you rent an apartment. Try to give yourself as many options as possible to leave. Don't sign a two-year lease, for example. When you get married, make it clear in advance what you want (maybe one side wants kids and the other doesn't) and how you can resolve these issues. This is not the same as a prenuptial agreement (which is purely financial) but an understanding of what both sides want (communication is always good in a marriage) and an understanding of how it can be resolved if wants and desires change (i.e., options to leave or change the nature of the relationship).

Sometimes there are not that many options you can negotiate. That's OK. Just remember the line "options equal freedom." In some cases, you may want to sell your freedom if the price is right.

For me, there is no price that is worth sacrificing freedom. But not everyone is the same.

If someone says, "you can be CEO of Google but you have to work fourteen hours a day for five years or we take all the money back," you may think that is an OK sacrifice for your freedom. Or not. But until you sign, you have the option.

This seems like a contradiction. Most people think, "More money equals more freedom."

There's a balance. You don't want to be a slave to your bills and debts. But you don't want to be a slave to massive downside either. Everything in life is about having as many options as possible so you can maximize your freedom. "Options" are not the same as "money."

Don't let cognitive biases limit your options when you make decisions. If you spend $400,000 and twelve years of your life learning how to become a brain surgeon, you now have this *huge* cognitive bias that you *must* be a brain surgeon.

This is not true. Maybe after all that, you decide you don't want to be a surgeon anymore. Make sure you can *always* list your options. Don't allow yourself to become trapped.

THINK, "IT'S NOT ME, BUT WHAT I CAN DO FOR YOU

When you negotiate, you always are bringing something to the table. But the negotiation is not about what you own. It's about the value you can deliver to the other person. The negotiation should be about whoever is bringing the higher value to the table.

As an extreme example, let's say you are selling your technology to Google. You've invested $5 million in the technology. They offer you $10 million. This seems great, right?

You counter: With this technology, you can generate an extra billion in profits every year! Now the negotiation is about that billion and not about your $5 million.

If they say, no, then no problem. You say, "OK, let's just work together." And you keep your options open while you talk to other companies and they start to get nervous you might sell to someone else.

Remember: the negotiation should *always* take place on the side where the higher value is. Unless the "secret options" discussed below take precedence. Which leads me to

---

Know That Infinite Patience Brings Immediate Results

Note that "infinite patience" and "immediate" seem to refer to time. But they don't. There is no unit of time called "immediate" and no unit of time called "infinite." When you have to deal with time in a negotiation, then you lose—if a negotiation has to be done by tomorrow, for instance, or next month.

If you can have infinite patience, then the negotiation will work out. And whether it works out immediately or not won't matter. You will have immediate results anyway.

We don't know what those results will be. But infinite patience means that whatever happens next will all take place according to plan. New suitors may show up. The negotiation might finish. Or something new altogether might happen. Your only goal is to structure your life and business and opportunities so that you can always have that infinite patience. Then the results will *always* be immediate.

Negotiate With Your Gut

Many people think that the brain is where all of the reasoning happens. It's true that this is where you calculate math, make logical assumptions, and draw logical well-thought out conclusions from your observations. But your gut and your heart have just as many neurons as the brain. It's really all one big intelligence system). Your gut doesn't say yes or no. But it does tell you when you are feeling good or bad about something.

Practice listening to your gut. If someone invites you to a meeting of the Ku Klux Klan, then your gut will feel pain even faster (I hope) than your head will. That's an extreme example, of course. But your gut is very much involved in every negotiation you do. So you have to practice paying attention to it.

Most people don't—so they make their negotiations with their brain and their gut gets less practice and therefore, less effective. One way to practice is to try not to do anything today where you feel even the slightest twinge in your gut that this might be wrong.

See what then happens. This is how you learn to trust your gut or at least build a better connection between the gut and the brain. Let's say someone invites you to a meeting and you feel a twinge. "But," your brain might say, "You *have* to go this meeting. Your boss will be there." Pay attention to the twinge. Maybe you are not prepared enough. Maybe you think it will be a waste of time. Maybe you have other things to do.

Everything is a negotiation. Make your list of reasons why you can't go bigger than the list of why you can. Negotiate your way out of the meeting. Listen to your gut just as much as you listen to your brain, if not *more*.

IMPORTANT: 95% of your serotonin (the neurochemical for happiness) is in the gut and not the brain. So in many cases, the decisions of your gut are much more important for your overall happiness. DNA doesn't care about happiness. The only goal of DNA is to replicate itself. But my guess is you care about your happiness.

NEGOTIATE WITH YOUR HEART

I only negotiate with people I like. What is the point of living otherwise?
Let's say you have to negotiate with the IRS. Like most people, I don't particularly like the IRS. But I recognize that the people there are just doing their jobs. And I can help them do their jobs by doing a good negotiation with them. On a bigger scale, there is no sense in selling a company or a service to someone you don't like.

Both sides will feel remorse. Both sides will be unhappy. And then they will die at some point. A bad negotiation is a cancer of the soul.

Be Aware of The Secret Negotiation

There are really two things components to every negotiation: the visible negotiation and then all the things that are hidden.

Maybe you are selling your company. But you might be buying your freedom (if you get a lot of money for your company). Or if you are getting a book advance, the secret thing (author Hugh McLeod calls this "your evil plan") might be that you feel that publishing a book will get you speaking opportunities, since most books don't make a lot of money. Always make sure that a negotiation gives you secret options. Remember: options equal freedom. Research your secret options thoroughly. Or else don't begin the negotiation because you have not prepared properly.

Be Ridiculous

In their book *Think Like a Freak*, Stephen Dubner and Steven Levitt describe the negotiation that the rock band Van Halen would do with concert organizers. Van Halen had a clause in their contract that required that a jar of M&Ms be delivered to their hotel room at the beginning of a gig and that there would be *zero* brown M&Ms in the jar. Why would they do this? Are they just being "rock stars" with ridiculous demands?

The answer is interesting: If they get brown M&Ms in the jar, despite this rider in the contract, then they know that the concert organizers were probably not detailed in all the other thousands of things that go into concert preparation. This would be a bad sign for Van Halen and force them to pay closer attention to the details of the concert or even force them to abandon the concert altogether.

So throw some ridiculous things into your negotiation. Not only does this make your list bigger, but also it will allow you to test how much someone really wants you involved and the care and attention they will place on you once the negotiation is finished.

Renegotiate

Even the Ten Commandments were easily broken (Moses actually smashed them and had to go back up the mountain to get new and *different* ones.) Every day and every interaction is a negotiation. Just because you have a signed and sealed contract doesn't mean you can't break it.

I'm not encouraging you to act in an unethical way. But if you are unhappy and feel you cannot perform your fullest, then make sure you come equipped with two things: the new value you offer the other side (or a big list of value) and what you need to succeed in this value. People sometimes seem unreasonable. But if you start off with the suggestions I've laid out here, then when it comes time to renegotiate—which happens in 90 percent of situations—then everyone will continue to be reasonable.

Particularly if you are staying physically, emotionally, mentally, and spiritually healthy, which allows you at all times to negotiate with your gut, heart, and brain instead of just the overworked brain.

"But is it against the law to break a contract?", you might wonder.

No. Because the value you bring is constantly changing and the world needs to be adjusted. All contracts can be broken if both sides agree that the world has changed. And the more options you have, the more the world will change in ways that are positive for both sides.

Prepare Everything; Script Nothing

Make sure you know all of your numbers. All of your lists of wants. All of the other side's numbers. All similar deals in your industry. All similar deals that the other negotiator has done. As many examples of negotiation, particularly in this arena, that you can find.

Then make sure you are negotiating from a position of strength. People usually think that means, "I have more power than you." But this is *not* what strength is. That will only result in a bad negotiation that will satisfy nobody in the long run. Strength simply means physical health (you're well slept, you've eaten well, you feel energy), emotional health (you are dealing with people you like), mental health (you have done your preparation), and spiritual health (you feel fully deserving of the abundance and gratitude that is coming your way).

Having faith in your strength is all you need to bring to the table. Nothing else. Once you do your preparation, have faith that the right negotiation will happen.

REMEMBER THAT THE BEST NEGOTIATION IS NO NEGOTIATION

I read recently that "in a good negotiation, both sides end up unhappy." I strongly disagree with this. That's a *horrible* negotiation. In a good negotiation, both sides don't even realize they were negotiating. They have just made a wonderful change to improve their lives and enhance the value they offer the people around them.

Don't forget the bigger picture: that you get a chance to love what you do and to live life as gently as possible, which gives you the energy to love what you do. You don't need to read all the self-help books on how to "win" a negotiation. There is no winning or losing. We're all negotiating with the universe around us every single second, as you are even right now as you read this.

The good news is, the universe wants us to win and has given us the sun, air, the ground, and all the people around us whom we love so we have the best opportunity to succeed.

Now . . . don't blow it.

USING IDEAS TO CONNECT PEOPLE: BUILDING A PERMISSION NETWORK

T he old rules and way of life made people ask, "How can I get ahead?" The new rules compel us to ask: "How can I help *others* get ahead?" Connecting people who can benefit each other is the most useful skill you can have on the entrepreneurial ladder of skills. When you help others make money by connecting them together, the world forces itself into the Möbius strip of success that brings the money right back to you times ten.

Some billionaires are especially great at this. If I write Mark Cuban an e-mail he responds in two seconds, even though he doesn't even know me. He's a "super connector." I know quite a few talented super connectors and they will be very successful as they grow into future Mark Cubans.

I love meeting new people. I've always done a good job with the initial skills involved with meeting new people. I feel like I can meet anyone in the world that I want to. Whether I make use of that meeting is another story (I'll expand on the importance of following up later).

You build a network by:

- Introducing people to others who can provide value for them. Make sure it's "permission networking" (you get permission from both sides first. Otherwise, you are a burden and not a help).
- Introducing people to ideas without any expectation of receiving something back. This means you have to get good at coming up with ideas.
- Finding a meaningful connection between you and the other person. A connection that person might value. Lewis Howes contacted many former ath-

letes. Sometimes people use their hometowns or schools. Sometimes people use mutual friends, etc.

Eight Skills You Need to Become a Super-Connector

1. **Introduce two other connectors.** If you can introduce two people who are themselves great connectors, then you become a meta-connector. They will meet and get along, since connectors get along with one another for two reasons: they are naturally friendly people (hence their ability to connect so easily with people) and they have a lot of friends in common almost by definition.

    If you are in the middle of that connection, then the two people will always remember you and you'll always be on their mind for future potential connections they can make that would be useful for you. And their Rolodexes are immense. So if you need to meet Prince William or Ellen Degeneres, for instance, then just connect two connectors and the next thing you know you'll be dancing right down the aisle with Ellen on her show or bowing to Kate Middleton, or whatever you want to do.

2. **Introduce two people,** but this time with a specific idea in mind. Marsha, meet Cindy. Cindy, meet Marsha. Marsha, you are the best book editor in the world. Cindy, your book is the best book idea I have ever heard. You both can make money together. No need to "cc" me.

    If you can help two other people make money, then eventually good things will happen to you. In a few cases, I've been able to do this. They're rare, but it's happened

    The first time I ever did this, back in 1994, I went home and told my girlfriend, "I just helped two people make money for the first time ever." And she said, "Yeah, but what did you get?" Well, I got nothing. But I *felt* something. I felt like I had done good in the world and that if I kept doing it, eventually it would return to me. And it did. With those very two people from that first time, but years later.

3. **HOST A DINNER OF INTERESTING PEOPLE.** I've only done this twice. When the last *Star Wars* prequel came out I invited people from every aspect of my life (friends, hedge fund investors, writers) to a dinner, I got everyone movie tickets, and it was a fun night. I solidified my relationships with some of my investors, plus some of the funds I was invested in, and I managed to connect people who later did business together. On another occasion I threw a party for everyone who had been fired by TheStreet. It got a little awkward when the guy who had done most of the firing (who had himself been fired right before the party) was also there—but it was all in good fun. I'm not sure how much goodwill it created for me. It's early to tell. I much more enjoy going to the dinner that I'm invited to. I've met a lot of interesting people. My main problem is that my normal bedtime is about 8 p.m. So sometimes I fall asleep at the table and everyone thinks I'm on drugs.

4. **FOLLOW UP.** This is the hardest part for me. I have a five-year-old list of people who introduced me to people I actually *wanted* to be introduced to and then I never followed up. For instance, a few months ago I wrote a post called "Burton Silverman, are you dead yet??" Burton Silverman is one of my favorite artists. I wanted to know if he was dead to see if the value of one of his paintings had gone up. He wrote me to tell me he wasn't dead yet. And as I type this, his studio is only a few blocks away. I could visit him right now if I want. Except for some reason I never returned his e-mail. He's on my list. But following up is the hardest part for me. Then I put it off until I start to feel guilty about not following up. So then I push back the follow-up even more.

At my first company I hired someone to follow up for me. Claudia has offered to follow up for me on e-mails. But I have a hard time letting other people do things for me that I should really be doing for myself. So learn from my area of weakness. If you make a connection, it's so easy to keep it by just saying, "Hey, it was great meeting you. Let's do that again in a month or so." Why the hell can't I ever do easy things?

5. **REESTABLISH CONTACT.** The other day I was following my own advice. I wrote an e-mail to an ex-investor of mine from 2004, saying sincerely how grateful I was he invested with me and I always enjoyed his advice and friendship. He immediately wrote back (because, unlike me, he's a good connector and businessman) and said, "What are you up to? Here's what I'm doing. Maybe we can work together again." This was six years after I'd last spoken to him.

6. **SHOW UP.** I don't know which rule on this list is the most valuable. But if a good connector invites you to a dinner or a meeting, then the best thing you can do is show up. I was invited to a party of forty bloggers the other night. The guy doing the inviting was Michael Ellsberg, who recently wrote the best-seller *The Education of Millionaires*. I probably should've gone. But 9 p.m.! That's past my bedtime! But chances are you go to bed a little later than I do. So when someone invites you to a gathering that starts at 9 p.m., show up.

7. **INTERVIEW PEOPLE.** Back to Michael Ellsberg, who did something genius. He figured he wanted to meet a lot of successful people, sort of the way Napoleon Hill did when he wrote his famous best-seller *Think and Grow Rich*. So Ellsberg got himself a book deal about how millionaires are educated and then, book deal in hand, he interviewed as many millionaires and billionaires as he could find. The guy is now a *mega*-connector. When I met him a few weeks ago, he had nonstop ideas about how one goes about meeting people. He should give conferences or do coaching on this one aspect alone. I've employed this technique—well, to some extent. It was always easy when I was writing for the *Wall Street Journal* or *Financial Times* to get people on the phone or meet me for breakfast. But—what else is new?—I had a hard time following up. Don't be like me! Follow up. Return calls. Return e-mails. Keep

connecting!

8. PRODUCE SOMETHING OF VALUE. In order to connect two people, you must have people to connect. You have to meet them in the first place, and the best way to do that is to produce something of value. I tell a story where I describe how when I was broke and about to go homeless I tried a technique of just reaching out to people. I would write letters like, "Hey, would love to meet." Unfortunately, that never worked. People are busy. Nobody wanted to meet some random guy like me.

So instead I tried a new technique. I would spend time researching the business of each person I wanted to meet and come up with ten ideas to help them that I would give them completely for free. I gave one guy, Jim Cramer, ten article ideas he should write. He ultimately wrote back, "You should write these"—which started my financial writing career. It also led to a habit of exchanging ideas with people at TheStreet that ultimately led to me selling Stockpickr to them. Another guy to whom I gave several trading system ideas ultimately allocated money for me to trade. This started my hedge fund trading career. Once I started concentrating on producing something of value—without worrying about what I would get out of it—it started coming back to me. Pretty amazing, huh?

DEVELOPING HABITS FOR ABUNDANCE

HOW TO MASTER ANYTHING

This chapter is about achieving mastery, but also why it's OK to not get mastery in the traditional sense. You can define it for yourself; you can avoid the definitions provided by everyone else. In other words, it's fine to be a loser.

There are a lot of books written on this topic. If you want to read one, try Robert Greene's *Mastery* (or listen to my podcast with him). There's also *Outliers,* by Malcolm Gladwell.

But it doesn't take a book to describe what makes a master. For one thing, most of us, and I mean me, will not be masters at anything. I try. I tried with chess. I hit the rank of "master," but that doesn't mean anything, since I'll never be world class at it. I've tried with writing. I've been writing for twenty or so years. I've known a lot of people who are among the best in the world in their field. I've talked to people and dissected what they thought led them to their mastery. I've built and sold businesses to people who were masters of their fields in every industry. I've invested in people who were masters in their fields. So I've at least recognized who were masters and what they did. So take this advice with a grain of salt—but know that it is based on my experience and the experiences of all the people with whom I've interacted. Here are the elements of mastery, and they involve both good news and bad news.

Having a Talent

I hate to say it, but talent is a factor. There's a myth that everyone is talented at doing at least one thing and you just have to find it. This isn't true.

Most people are not truly talented at anything. However, most people can be *pretty good* at something. For instance, author Timothy Ferris shows in his book *The Four-Hour Chef* how you can be a pretty good chef with four hours' worth of work. I've tried his techniques, and in four hours I made some pretty good dishes. Thank you, Tim. But at the launch of Tim's book he held a dinner where each course (I think there were eight of them) was cooked by a different chef. One of the chefs was (approximately) eight years old and his dish might've been the best served. That kid will be a master one day if he isn't already. That's *talent*. And that's the difference.

When my chess ranking was peaking back in 1997 I played in a tournament against a girl fittingly named Irina Krush. She really did crush me in about twenty-five moves. After the match she told me, "Maybe your bishop to B4 move felt a little weak to me." She was right. She was thirteen years old. I stopped playing chess in tournaments right that moment and now only play when I'm on the phone with people. She had talent. She's now one of the youngest women grand masters in the world.

Finding What You're Talented At

I think there are roughly two methods for doing this:

1. **Take out a pad.** List everything you enjoyed doing from the ages of six to eighteen, before your life was ruled by college, relationships, crappy jobs, mortgages, kids, responsibilities, self-loathing, etc.

   Lewis Howes, whom I introduced in a prior chapter, mentioned he had always wanted to be an athlete since he was a little kid. He also mentioned that he used networking skills to help himself out even at an early age in order to deal with what seemed like poor academic skills. He found his two talents and became masters at both.

Often, it's a combination of sub-talents that make you uniquely a master in that one field. I don't know if I will ever master anything, but since I was a kid I have loved writing, games, and anything to do with business. So I've combined some of those and done what I think is pretty well. Maybe one day I'll master something. We'll see.

2. **GO TO THE BOOKSTORE.** Find a topic you would be willing to read five hundred books on. If you can't wait to read all five hundred books in the knitting section, then you probably have a talent for knitting. (Note that it is really OK not to be talented in the arts or with crafts. Most us weren't put on this earth to be talented at knitting.)

We ultimately are a combination of all of our experiences, all of the things we are interested in, all of the things we flirt with. And that combination might look like garbage to everyone else. So play with your garbage and be happy. If you can do that, you're in the top 0.00001 percent.

DOING THAT THING FOR FOUR HOURS A DAY

There is a reason that the titles of all of Tim Ferriss's books start with *The Four-Hour...* I ask almost every master I encounter, in every field, how much time per day they spend mastering their field. They never give the standard Silicon Valley BS entrepreneur answer: "I work twenty hours a day and if I didn't need to sleep I'd work thirty hours a day." You can't get good at something if you are working twenty hours a day. In fact, something is very wrong in your life if that is how much you are working at *one* thing.

The typical answer is "I study four hours a day." Former world chess champion Anatoly Karpov said the maximum he would study chess is three hours a day. Then, when he wasn't in tournaments, he'd spend the rest of the day exercising, studying languages, and doing other things to balance out his life.. If you just do one thing, the benefits quickly decline and you also ignore the pleasure of becoming well-rounded. Ultimately, mastery is about connecting the dots of many fields. So while you can focus for only so long on your field of choice, it's often of great benefit to learn other areas of life.

Prominent behavioral psychologist Dan Ariely has done research that tells us that the peak productivity period in a person's day is 2-5 hours after they wake up. After that, he says, there are declining returns on the work you put in.

KNOWING THE HISTORY

In any area of life you want to succeed at, you have to study the history.
All art is created in context. If someone wrote Beethoven's Fifth Symphony right now it would be laughed at. It wouldn't fit the context of today's popular music, even though it would be a work of genius. Andy Warhol tried many different approaches before he decided that art based on things like Campbell's soup cans was the right art for the right moment in time. Studying the history of how previous world champions played and trained in any sport is critical toward figuring how you can improve on that training and playing.

In any business, studying the history of your focus industry, the biographies of the prior executives, and the successes and failures of those who went before you is critical for mastering that business.

For example, I had Greg Zuckerman (author of the best selling book "The Frackers") on my podcast to talk about the current resurgence in oil drilling in the United States. Everyone thought the United States was out of oil back in the 1970s. Well, now the fastest-growing city in the United States is Williston, North Dakota, and the United States will probably be a net energy exporter by 2020.

Heck, the one McDonald's in Williston has gone from $5 million in revenues to $18 million in revenues last year. (The average McDonald's does $8 million in revenues.)

If I were remotely interested in fracking I'd study where all the oil was drilled back in the 1920s, '50s, '70s. How the first wildcatters found their wells. What technologies they used and the history of the technology. How they made improvements. I'd ask, what's the history of the geopolitics around oil drilling? And so on. Somewhere in there, there is a path to getting incredibly wealthy. Not for me, because I could care less about oil. But for someone. Or many someones.

STUDYING YOUR FAILURES

I was once talking to poker champ Ylon Schwartz, who has won over $7 million in tournaments and untold millions in informal cash games. We grew up together playing chess until he made the switch first to backgammon and then poker. I asked him why a lot of people play poker for twenty years but never get better.

He said, "Everyone wants to blame someone. They want to blame bad luck. Or they had a fight with their wife. But the key is to study your failures. You have to take notes about your losing hands and even your winning hands. You have to think about *everything*."

We spoke about another friend of ours who went from homeless to millionaire in six months, once he found that he had a knack for backgammon. His nickname was Falafel because that was once all he could afford to eat.

Ylon told me, "Falafel memorized every statistic about backgammon. Right now on the Web you can see that his tournament games are ranked number one in terms of how accurately they mimic a computer. Falafel also studied every single game he lost."

I used to play Falafel every day in chess. He'd sleep on the ground in Washington Square Park and get up in the morning with dirt and leaves in his hair and we'd play chess for fifty cents a game. Now million-dollar paydays from backgammon are normal for him.

———— ⊱⊰ ————

GAINING EXPERIENCE

At some point you have to cook 10,000 meals. Or play a million hands of poker. Or a thousand of games of chess. Or start twenty businesses. Very few are successful right away. That would require too much luck, and luck favors the prepared and the persistent.

In those thousands of repetitions of whatever, you will encounter much failure. Those familiar with baseball know that the best hitters in the world are enormous successes if they are called out "only" 70 percent of the times they go to bat.

A lot of people can play the 10,000 hands of poker and never get better. Or bake a thousand cakes and never get better. You have to remember your experiences, study your failures, try to note what you did right and what you did wrong, and remember it all for future experiences.

Future experiences will almost never be exactly like the old experiences. But they give you the ability to say, "Hmm, this is like the time four years ago when X, Y, and Z happened." And then you are engaging in . . .

———— ⊱⊰ ————

USING PATTERN RECOGNITION

Being able to recognize when current circumstances are like an experience you've had in the past or an experience *someone else* you've studied had in the past is critical to mastery.

Pattern recognition is a combination of all of the above: study + history + experience + talent + a new thing . . . love.

———— ⊱⊰ ————

Loving It

Andre Agassi has famously said he doesn't love tennis. I believe this and I don't believe it. We all know that there are all kinds of love. There's unconditional love, which is very hard to maintain. Then there's lust. You look at someone and she is the *oomph* to your *ugh*. She is the *BAM!* to your *BOOM!* You dream and daydream and dream and daydream until the love is all worn out, and six months or six years later it's over and you move on.

Then there's love that matures. There's a set of things you like about a person, even love. Mix that in with some lust. Then this love mash-up changes over time. Or you learn to adapt because you know that a maturing love is not one where you settle or explore the subtleties inside the other person but you are finally able to explore the subtleties inside of yourself.

And sometimes you just fall out of love. There is no shame in this. Do what your heart tells you to do. Some relationships are weird combinations of all of the above. They are tumultuous. There is much pain and much pleasure. Perhaps tennis was like that for Agassi.

But to become a master at anything there has to be love—so there will inevitably be much pain. And it can't be avoided. Nobody has avoided it.

If something is too painful, then it's not the worst thing in the world to give up. I don't like dental surgery. It's too much pain for me. So my teeth are messed up a bit. I give up on having perfect teeth.

Applying Positive Psychology

One reason most people in the world don't get really good at anything is because they have no talent for anything that anyone cares about. Another reason is they don't want to put in the work. This is understandable. Often it's better to be social and have friends and strong family relationships and love people.

When you have a career, there's this idea that you will go from one success to the next. You start in the cubicle, then you get an office, then a corner office, then you move horizontally into a CEO position at another company, and so on. You might have some failures along the way but they won't be big failures. But when it comes to mastery, there are *always* big failures.

The day before poker champ Ylon Schwartz left for Las Vegas in 2008—where he won over $3 million—I was with him, providing support for him in a court case. He had a court-appointed attorney because he was dead broke and in debt. He asked me that day, "I have to get on a plane for Las Vegas tomorrow and when I get back I could go to jail. How am I going to get through this?" I didn't have an answer for him other than the usual clichés. But he got on that plane. And every day he went higher and higher in chips. And he won $3.7 million in that tournament and hasn't looked back.

When I was at my worst, the first thing I had to do was convince myself that I could succeed again. Then, and only then, could I take the first step back—the tiniest step that would release me from my fears and anxieties and allow me to move forward, if not to mastery, then at least to success.

On the path to mastery, everything will go wrong.

As Robert Greene points out in his book, Napoleon got banished to Elba, where he supposedly said his famous palindrome (somehow speaking English for the first and only time in his life) "Able was I ere I saw Elba"

Every master has his Elba. Banished to an island where the life you once knew no longer exists and it seems like there is no way to escape. Napoleon escaped because he was the best in the world at what he did. Because he had the psychology, or perhaps the blind spot, to not recognize that this was it, his final destination. The story of how he came back to power offers a great study in psychology and exemplifies the skills required of a master.

Bobby Fischer spent much of his life in borderline schizophrenic agony when he couldn't deal with his losses. He'd disappear for years at a time but then come back stronger than ever.

How do you build that psychology? I don't know. It's a combination of a few things, including:

- **EGO.** Real belief that you can be the best, against all possible rational evidence to the contrary, against everyone trashing you simultaneously.
- **REALIZING THAT THERE'S A WAY OUT.** I've asked Ylon, Lewis, and many others what were they thinking at rock bottom and the answer almost always was something like "What else could I do with my life? I had to keep going!"

Which leads us to…

———∞———

HAVING PERSISTANCE

Add up all of the above and you get persistence. Persistence creates luck. Persistence gets you experience. Persistence is a sentence of failures punctuated by the briefest of successes, and eventually those successes will start to propel you toward mastery. Not one success or two. But many, many, many.

How do you keep persisting when life is filled with changing careers, relationships, responsibilities, economic crashes, historical upswings, and so many things that can get in your way?

There's no answer. That's why it's called persistence. Because no matter where you are, there you are, doing what you always did. Not letting any of the above stop you. Using all of the above in your mastery arsenal to propel you to higher successes (if sometimes also deeper failures) and then even higher successes. It's painful and brutal and no fun and nobody will ever understand why. And when you achieve success people will act as if it's the most natural thing in the world to have happened to you.

And you try to explain, "No, there was this one time . . ." but they don't want to hear it. They want to know what their next move should be so they can be where you are. There's no next move. There's only your next move.

So you can only do this:

Ask, "What can I do right now to move forward, in this second?" Having a goal in the distant future is almost a damnation of this moment in time. An insult. We can't predict the future. And the history of mastery shows that nobody was able to predict which goals would work and which wouldn't. Only this moment matters. Health-wise: physically, emotionally, mentally, and spiritually. Can you move forward today in each area? Then you will attract mastery.

THE GOOD NEWS

You don't have to be the master of the world. You don't have to do any of the above. Very few people do. And many of them experienced much hardship and pain along the way. And will continue to experience that hardship.

We live in a culture where it's almost a damnation to be considered mediocre. But society has no clue about what real mastery is. Freud has said that our two goals in life are human connection and achievement. But often it's a reasonable goal to overcome these evolutionary inclinations. To be happy with your loved ones. To be satisfied for every gift in your life, for every moment, not rushing to the next moment of mastery. True mastery can be found right here, right now.

Choosing yourself right now in how you treat yourself, how you treat the people around you, how you treat your efforts and your loves. Nothing is more important than this. Nothing compounds into greater happiness in life than this. Because when you rush to get to a mythical *there*, one day you will arrive and realize you missed all of the pleasures and mysteries along the way.

GETTING RID OF YOUR EXCUSES

There were many times over many years where the only thing I was abundant in was excuses. I was too ugly to meet a beautiful woman. I didn't have any money so couldn't start a business. And even if I started one, I didn't have an office, or clients, and I was too shy to cold-call clients.

I didn't have talent. Nobody was going to hire me. I didn't have the right equipment.

I couldn't write a book because I had no publisher. I couldn't do stand-up because I was afraid people would heckle me. I was often afraid to write blog posts, because what would people think of my ideas?

All of my excuses turned out to be blessings in disguise. There's *always* a gap between "what I have now" and "what I would like." And that gap is all of your excuses. All it takes to close the gap is to be creative and work your way through the excuses. I repeat: this is *all it takes.*

Following are some of the types of excuses that I've used in the past and still haven't quite completely let go of. You should make your own list, because no one knows your excuses better than you do. In this way, excuses are the map to success and fulfillment. It's fun to take a blank piece of paper and draw out the map. Label the roads, mountains, buildings, rivers, obstacles, and destinations.

I DON'T HAVE ENOUGH MONEY

When I started my first business, called Reset, (we made websites for entertainment companies) I had no money in the bank at all. And I had a very low salary at HBO. Oh, and I had a full-time job. It was brutal. I had to get very creative about finding computers to use and reaching out to friends and family to tell them what my skill set was and what sorts of clients would be great for me (Answer: anyone who needed *anything*, I would help for a fee). So my solution was to make sure *everyone* knew what my skills were and why they were needed. Then I carved out time (weekends, nights, days when I could hide) to do the work for clients until I was ready to jump to being a full-time entrepreneur (by that point, my company was up to having about ten employees).

I Don't Have The Equipment

A friend and I recently spoke about people doing YouTube videos who are making a living from all the views and advertising they generate. He claimed, "I'd do it but I don't have the right camera." I said to him, "You want to borrow my phone? Because any phone in the world has a camera a thousand times better than what you need for YouTube." I asked him what else was getting in the way. "There's always a good reason and the *real* reason," I told him. "You just gave me a bullshit good reason. What do you think the real reason is?" And he thought about it and told me. "Laziness." I get that. I'm lazy also. "So take your phone camera. And practice executing. Pick an easy video to do. Go to the Forty-Second Street subway and videotape the guys playing underground there and upload it. Just get into the rhythm of making a video and uploading it. Then, write down ideas every day about more and more fun videos you can do. It's a quantity game."

Will he do it? I don't know. We love our excuses. They are just as much our babies as our ideas are.

I Don't Have The Time

Let's say you are a single mother with three kids and a full-time job. You might think you don't have time to write *Harry Potter*. But you give it a try anyway.

It's really harsh, but you find the time. You stop watching TV. Or skip a meal. (Nobody in America will ever starve by skipping a meal. I will put my medical seal of approval on that statement.) The magic of excuses is that there is always a way to be creative around them. We all have obstacles. You can view the obstacle as an opportunity to grow or as a reason to stop. You get to choose.

I'm Not Good Enough

When I had *New York Observer* sex columnist Jasmine Lobe on my podcast, we talked about Kamal Ravikant's approach when he was sick. He would look in the mirror and say "I love myself" over and over again. He might not have believed it at first. But repeating it, as he put it so eloquently in his book, "rewired his brain."

I told Jasmine I would do the same (and here is my excuse), but I hate looking at myself in the mirror. She said, "Why don't you look in the mirror and repeat, 'I am handsome' until your brain is rewired." I haven't done it yet. But maybe one day I will.

I Don't Have a Degree

I get e-mails every day. "I'd like to work at Google but I don't have degree." Or, "I'd like to be a success but I don't have an MBA."

And it's not just degrees. I get e-mails from people who think they need yoga teacher certification. Or a medical degree (you can be a healer without writing prescriptions). Or any flimsy piece of paper that ultimately is no indicator of value. Google's head of HR has even announced that graduates' GPAs are a waste to look at. And that more and more of their hires have no college degrees at all! It's just another way the world is changing, and you have to grasp it now. It used to be that a stranger knew he could cooperate with you if you had that stupid piece of paper. But now there are many ways you can show you can deliver value *without* that paper. Come up with ten ideas on how you can escape the trap of the degree and demonstrate you still have value. Ideas for the company you want to work for, or the person you want to work with. Or just go get a camera and start making movies without a film degree.

When actor Andy Samberg was starting at *Saturday Night Live* he didn't just huddle in the writers' room with everyone else and try to come up with jokes. There was too much competition! Instead, he took a camera and with his buddies Jorm and Akiva went out and shot "Lazy Sunday," which was the first YouTube video to get over 100 million views and became his first SNL digital short. He didn't wait to rise through the ranks and hopefully get a joke or a sketch produced. He went out and produced it himself.

Before Macklemore's "Thrift Shop" got a billion views on YouTube, the rapper turned down every record label. He realized he didn't need the validation they have provided to generations of artists. The distribution is there to reach the world no matter what your field is. You validate yourself now through your work.

⸗∞⸗

I'm Not in The Right Location

I moved from Pittsburgh to New York because I thought it would put me closer to the publishing industry. Some people move to Silicon Valley to get funding for their start-up. I once had a friend who felt she needed to live in Paris before she could paint. I know *many* people who think they need to own a home before they can really have roots and start creating.

All of these are good reasons, but they are not the real reasons. What affects whether people will get to see your work is not where you live but if you actually *do* the work. When I built stockpickr.com, I spent less than five thousand dollars and virtually never left my basement, eighty miles north of NYC. Oh, I was afraid all the time. It was the tenth website I had tried to launch, and the prior nine had failed. I had no idea if it would be good or bad. It kept breaking down (I couldn't afford good programmers), one employee working on it quit (because I couldn't pay him), and I realized too late that it had three or four decent competitors. But eventually it took off and in the second month had almost a million visitors and then kept growing until I sold it to TheStreet just five months later.

It didn't make a difference where I did it, because I loved doing it. I wanted to create what would be the ideal site for someone like me interested in finance. So it worked. No matter that I was in a dark basement the entire time with no money.

———⊗∞∞⊗———

I Don't Have The Right Network

I am a bad cold-caller. When I was launching my first business I cold-called a bank and asked them if I could do their website. My only "in": I said I had a checking account there. They laughed and told me to call them back in a few years.

A few years! I had a payroll to make!

Lewis Howes described to me how he would make all of these LinkedIn connections and then invite them all out to open-bar parties where they could network.

He created his network by introducing *everyone else* to one another. He was simply that guy in the middle.

You want to be "that guy." We covered some of this in the chapter on networking, but here are a few more tips.

Building a network from scratch requires three to four hours a day of work. What if you have a job? Well, build your network at work. Ask to lunch the assistants of people in different divisions. Come up with ideas for the heads of different divisions. Do one thing a day to help someone in your work group that you didn't have to reach out to. Networks build exponentially and not linearly.

Once one person is in your network—*one single person*—then everyone in their network is potentially in yours. Make use of that.

"I don't have a network" is a beautiful excuse because it means that if you overcome this excuse you are going to meet many amazing friends whom you will know and love throughout your career. I know this because my "network" has changed 100 percent in the past five years, starting from total scratch. Every day I bow down to how powerful this one excuse was to motivate me into making such great and wonderful new friends.

My Idea is Too Crazy

When he was about fifty years old (maybe even older), Rodney Dangerfield was an aluminum siding salesman. But he wanted to return to his old career as a stand-up comedian. It was crazy for him to think he could be a success. I don't know what was going through his head. But whatever it was, he did the smart thing. He opened up his own comedy club. Dangerfield's. It became the most popular comedy club in NYC, and many famous comedians—including people like Jim Carrey—got their start there. Who would deny Dangerfield if he wanted to go on stage there? He developed his craft more and more until he was basically the most obscene movie star ever.

A. J. Jacobs wants to create the world's largest family reunion. Over 4,000 people. That's crazy! But every day he takes tiny steps closer to his goal. (For one thing, we found out through DNA testing that we are cousins, as are his wife and I!). He also found a venue. A publisher is going to publish a book about it. He's getting sponsors. Every day, there are new answers to the "That's crazy!" excuse.

Dr. Wayne W. Dyer had a tenure track position at a college. He was in his late thirties. He was set for life. But he quit, loaded up the back of his car with copies of a self-help book he'd published, and drove across the country leaving his books at every bookstore. Everyone he knew thought he was crazy. He sold over a million copies of that book, *Your Erroneous Zones.*

Many things might be too crazy. But I've been in business on my own for twenty years now. I have helped over three hundred companies get financed. I've started and sold many companies (and gone broke many too many times).

I have seen the craziest things happen. People rise from unbelievably bleak and desperate ashes to be the one flower in a graveyard to blossom. The sun is always there. But the flower has to be ready to blossom. "That's crazy" is a roadmap. Start with that phrase and circle it. Then draw all the roads that lead out from that spot. They don't all have to end up at the place you expect. Have fun with it. Find different roads and see where they lead.

Some will end up in Oz. But some will end up in even more magical places than you could ever have imagined.

I Don't Have Talent

Neither did *Mick Jagger.* He had a weird voice and couldn't play an instrument. But he loved the blues and wanted to put his spin on it with the help of Keith Richards and others. And he worked it. It turned out he had this weird sort of charisma that kept the fans coming back.

Jagger never would've found that out if he hadn't played every night at the seedy underground clubs where he would bang out his horrible music. He would've finished his degree at the London School of Economics and become a respectable accountant somewhere. Instead, he's Mick Jagger.

It's widely agreed that the best chess player ever, Bobby Fischer, didn't have that much talent. He was above average but maybe not world class. He had to figure out his own particular roadmap to success. So he did three things:

1. HE STUDIED GAMES FROM THE 1800S and came up with improvements to each one. This way, when people played him and found them-

selves in positions he recognized from his studies, he would know the best moves to make and they wouldn't.

2. **HE LEARNED RUSSIAN** so he could read the Russian chess magazines to learn the latest openings that none of his US opponents knew.

3. **HE PLAYED SPEED CHESS** every day with his teacher, strong master Jack Collins.

Then he came out of nowhere (he had literally disappeared from the scene) and became the youngest US champion ever. Then the strongest player ever.

Remember to always tune your inner ear so you can listen for (and separate from each other) both the *good* reason and the *real* reason when anyone (including yourself) gives you an excuse. Most people don't tune their ear this way. They believe their own excuses because it's easier to do so. Because it gives them permission not to do something they love. I understand that, too. I give myself permission every day to miss out on some opportunities because I choose others. That's why on your roadmap of excuses, some excuses don't have many roads coming out of them. They don't need an extra traffic circle or bridge because their port is not in use much.

I know my children will have excuses as they climb each rung on the ladders of age, success, frustration, relationships, spirituality, and health. I want them to know that the best things that ever happened to me were my excuses. Each excuse let me learn about myself, let me discover entire worlds of surprising possibilities. Each one led me to more and more love. But I want my kids to not go through some of the pains that I have gone through. It really sucks to be so sad you don't know if you can last another day. To not have anything to grasp on to. The worst excuse is to say "It's all just luck," or "I'm just a fraud," and then to think you have no luck and you never will again. We choose our excuses. They don't choose us. But love comes when we kiss our excuses and, magically, they kiss back and feed the next stage of our lives.

May you have many, many excuses in your life.

WHY TO-DO LISTS DON'T WORK

So how on earth are you going to start all of this? Get all of these ideas out there? Get all of these people together? You're probably thinking, man, I need to make a to-do list.

But to-do lists don't work. To-do lists kill people. They will make you so stressed you will die an early death.

In 2003, I was just beginning a new career. I had lots of things to do every day. I was writing a few articles a day. I was day trading. I was selling a business. I was thinking of other businesses to start. And my dad had a stroke and died.

Well, it didn't happen that fast. The last time I had spoken to my dad I had hung up on him. He called back but I wouldn't pick up. He wrote every few months but I didn't respond. Then he had a stroke. Then he never spoke or moved again (he blinked) and then he died two years later. I would visit the hospital once a week and just sit there because I felt obligated to. I would turn on CNBC. Everything smelled bad. I'd feel sick to my stomach. Brain-dead dad in front of me, whom I hadn't spoken to when I could have, even though we had been close all my life. And I was losing money every second and maybe going broke. Again.

All of this is to say, I had so much to do that I tried keeping a to-do list to manage it all. Suffice it to say it didn't work.

You've likely heard the mantra that one must have goals. I don't live by goals. I don't have the goal, "do this by X date." I have a "theme" that I want to have a high quality of life until the day I die.

HAVE *THEMES* INSTEAD OF GOALS

To-do lists are very goal oriented. They are the exact opposite of achieving themes. Here are the simple reasons why I *never* use a to-do list.

∞

THEY CAUSE STRESS

The nature of a to do list is that every item on it is something I haven't done. For me (maybe not for you), the reason these items made the list is because I will feel stress until they are done. Items like "respond to Jimmy the Tool's e-mail."

Until the moment I hit send on an e-mail to Jimmy the Tool I will feel. deep down, "I have to write an e-mail to Jimmy the Tool" and a tinge of anxiety. Multiply that by twenty and that's real stress.

∞

THEY DON'T HIGHLIGHT IMPORTANCE

The reason I don't make a to-do list is because I know if I stick to my general themes of the day (be creative, be healthy, less stress, do things I love) I will naturally do the things that are important to me.

For instance, writing this book is important to me. Going to my kid's plays is the *worst thing in existence* (err, I mean, they are very important to me and I will be there). I know that if I live a healthy and creative life I will *automatically* always do the next thing that's important to me.

Someone could say, "Well what if you have a programmer job or some job that requires to-do lists?"

Well, I do feel I have a career like that. So try it. Create a theme of how you want to live your life. And then do the next thing that's important to you. It might be to take a nap. But I doubt it will be to watch the Kardashians.

∞

You Don't Know What Should Be on It

During the day I often end up doing things that are important that I would never have guessed were important to me. Like maybe getting a flower for Claudia. This would never appear on my to-do list but it might suddenly become important to me (if I accidentally spill coffee on her dress, for instance).

If I had a to-do list I might get even more stressed not getting to it. The to-do list becomes my master and I become the slave. One of my themes is "less slavery in my life."

I'd rather do the things that I realize are important that moment rather than some random BS I wrote down over a cup of coffee at six in the morning.

They Cause Disappointment

You're never going to do all the things on your to-do list. Most people put too much down on the to-do list. I bet most people only get done 50 percent of the things on their to-do lists.

Not only that, but people keep daily, weekly, yearly (i.e., New Year's resolutions) to-do lists.

That's a lot of things to do! When do you relax and enjoy life? You're going to die, you know.

When you die are you going to say, "Damn, I forgot to e-mail Jimmy the Tool," and then die?

Delegate

Try this: make your usual to-do list and then don't do anything on it. It's like a to-don't list.

Did the universe end? Now see how many of the things on your list you can delegate or just not do.

For instance, you can call Jimmy the Tool next week when things are a little less hectic. Or, heck, never call him again! Who cares about him?

"Things are never less hectic!" you might say. That's because you have too many to-do lists. Please trust me and try this. Things will get less hectic.

I'm not saying do *nothing*. I'm saying if you make themes of your life, you will always do what is important to you, your family, your friends, and so on. Themes ripple out to the farthest shores. To-do lists keep you anchored to the ocean floor. Also, your "to-don't" lists will point you in directions where you can delegate instead of "do".

࿎

THEMES ARE BETTER

I'm not saying do nothing. Try making a themes list instead. This way, you will always do what is important to you, your family, your friends, and so on. To-do lists keep you anchored to the ocean floor. Themes ripple out to the farthest shores. Also, your themes list will point you in directions where you can delegate instead of "do."

I like to check the box on being creative every day. And on the Daily Practice I advocate in my books and blog: physical, emotional, mental, and spiritual health. That's all. Those are my themes.

I have no idea what they will have me do today.

All that means (at a minimum) is that I like to sleep well, eat well, take a walk, be around people I enjoy, be creative every day, and be grateful every day. Then I know if I do that today, life will be a little better tomorrow.

So,

- Make a themes list. When you have themes, you build unbelievable intuition on what is the next thing you should be doing in your life. You're no longer trapped by a long list of tiny inconsequential things you feel you have to do.
- Make an "I Did It!" list.

The benefit of the "I Did It!" list is as follows: "I did it! And it felt great! Woo-hooo! I called five people by 11 a.m.!"

Accomplishment releases all kinds of chemicals in the brain that then make you feel better. Very addictive chemicals. Dopamine, endorphins, blah, blah. I'm not trying to be a productivity expert here, since I'm not very productive by traditional measures. I don't respond to e-mails very well and I don't use my phone or do all the things that people might expect me to do.

But I am writing several books, running two podcasts, and preparing for a third. And I also write every day. I love every minute of it. Even though I have to go to my kid's performances, I'll play backgammon on the iPad in the back of the room when it's not the kid's turn to speak or sing. I don't know if that makes me a good dad or bad dad.

My dad didn't go to any of my performances. But we'd play Ping-Pong every night. Or chess. And I suspect he sometimes would let me win when I would throw all the pieces on the floor in disgust. Or throw my paddle at him. Even when I was thirty-five years old.

Part 2
MAKING MONEY IN THE TWENTY-FIRST CENTURY

Trends: The Power to See Things Differently Than Everyone Else

I t's very special to me that you are reading this book. As you read this book, I'm reading it, too. I'm always rereading it, wondering what people think about different sections, concerned about whether I'm getting my message across.

The odds are, though, that if you've made it this far, then you want to keep going. That's good. This chapter is important, because it's going to highlight some of the big demographic trends that are sweeping across the twenty-first century. The last chapter gave you direction on how to develop habits and think about this new economy we're living in now. This chapter is going to get a little more specific, starting with identifying where a lot of those changes are taking place.

Trends are an interesting metaphysical topic for several reasons. For one thing, I strongly believe the key to success is to be calm today, since that's the best predictor of a successful day tomorrow. But that doesn't mean you stand on the edge of the beach when a hurricane is coming. You still have to do *right now* whatever it takes to ensure your survival, to make the moves that will help you and your family survive, and maybe even thrive for tomorrow.

The trends that are coming are that hurricane. When you notice a trend, you do so for several reasons:

- It might indicate what *stocks to buy.*
- It might indicate what businesses to start. And for every one trend there are many different *businesses you can start.*
- If it's a negative trend, it might suggest how you can *position your family to survive.*

- It gives you something to *talk about with your friends.*
- It gives you *ideas* that may morph into revenue streams that nobody has ever thought of before.

I will tell you that the way I make money is through the last item listed. I think of ideas for other companies who call me, and my "business" is to them help them implement those ideas on their own and become massive successes.

If you combine the ideas *that* trends give birth to with an understanding of demographic trends, there are trillions of dollars waiting to made.

Think about it: this entire book is about a trend, the end of corporatist America or the corporatist world where a handful of institutions and the people that ride them like wild horses are losing the power to make choices for you. Choices regarding what you make, what you eat, where you live, where you educate yourself, whom you marry, what you do to make money, what you do to find peace and happiness. And we know by now that that trend is ending for the reasons we discussed as early as the first chapter in this book.

The way you deal with end of that trend is by developing the skills of a successful artist/entrepreneur/world leader and using those skills to sculpt exactly the life you want. Without those skills, someone else will start making choices for you and ultimately you will have to live with someone else's choices and not your own. And that won't be pleasant.

A trend is a reflection that some way of life is ending and another way of life is beginning. For instance, Henry Ford could've said that the era of transportation by horse was ending, while that of the automobile was dawning.

No matter what the trend, a group of people will gather and complain. When Henry Ford was talking about his big trend, many people were happy, but then later many people were sad. For one thing, there was horse poo all over the street all the time. It was the end of the era of horse poo in the street. But now because we have to get to work and we live farther out in the suburbs, we need a lot of fuel that we dig out of the earth and then do something to and then spit into the air to get to work. People complain about that. Any time there is change, people will complain, and resist. Some people will always insist that the "old way" was better. But you and I know better.

Most of the trends I'll discuss are based on two important ideas:

1. ALL THINGS END, and the better we prepare for that end, the more our legacies will just be beginning.

2. INNOVATION TAKES PLACE NONSTOP. Humans didn't innovate for 2 million years, and then suddenly, with the arrival of the printing press, we began to innovate at faster and faster rates. Every year the level of innovation is higher than that of the year before.

So if you want to buffer yourself against everything you ever worry about, best to do so focusing on a trend that relates to one of the above two ideas.

TREND #1: BIOTECH

As you're probably aware, the baby boomers—members of the postwar generation born during the years 1946 to 1964—are aging. As of a few years back, 76 million boomers had hit the traditional retirement age, and—surprise—kept going. They kept playing tennis. They kept skydiving. And because of the nature of the economy, many of them kept working. But here are a few things that happen to lots and lots of people when they get older:

- They get dementia and Alzheimer's.
- They become more and more farsighted.
- They get lonely.

They look for cosmetic treatments to take care of the veins on their legs, or now-splotchy tattoos they had etched painfully into their skin years earlier that they now regret. They might look for new spouses after old ones get sick or die. Their children are no longer massive financial burdens on them, so they can finally spend some money on travel. Or a fiftieth or sixtieth anniversary. Or an eightieth-birthday party.

Another common but unfortunate event that occurs as we age is that a lot of us suffer from physical ailments and diseases like cancer. Everyone in the world has cancer cells in their body. You do and I do. Sometimes those cells aggregate together in such ways that it hurts us and we go see a doctor. The doctor says, "Oh my god, you have ten months to live."

I am constantly on the lookout for new ways to diagnose cancer. The currently most popular way is going to be replaced just as travel by horse was replaced by cars. Doctors do something called a biopsy, a surgery where they take some of your skin and blood, send it to a lab, and then call you while you anxiously await their call, and tell you the results. This is the old school approach.

Every day, I look for companies that are able to diagnose cancer faster and more efficiently than this old method. Tests are taking place at all the largest cancer research facilities in the world for testing cancer via your stools, your urine, and your DNA. I keep track of all of these tests. I go out and visit the facilities. I get doctors to explain the science to me. There are a few reasons for this. First of all, if I ever get cancer I want to know it right away.

When Steve Jobs first got cancer he decided to use alternative approaches to treat his cancer. I have nothing against alternative approaches. Some work and some don't. In his case, they did not work. When he finally got tested again, ten months later, he was in a much worse, more advanced stage of a dreadful sort of cancer, pancreatic cancer.

What if he could've tested himself at home every day instead of going in for a painful surgery? He would've known very quickly if the alternative treatments were working. With the tests going on now, I am sure Steve Jobs would still be alive.

How can you take advantage of this trend? For one thing, you can buy stocks of companies that are involved in these new technologies. This is not a stock recommendation book so I will leave the details for another time. You can write a newsletter about the latest technologies. There is a market closing in on 100 million people that would love to read about these technologies. You can use the technologies to perhaps create other companies to help people be aware of them.

In 1999, nobody knew how to value Internet companies. It was *very* clear to everyone that the Internet was going to be big. And everyone was right. Amazon and Apple have gone straight up in revenues since 1999. So have eBay and Priceline. For a while there was a bubble in fascination, in IPOs, about the Internet. But now Facebook has a billion customers and Twitter has 400 million users and everyone buys books and other products on amazon.com. The dream came true.

But because we didn't know how to value these companies, a strange thing happened on the corner of Wall Street and Broad Street. In a little building on that corner, the New York Stock Exchange, the prices of these companies went straight through the roof. When society as a whole doesn't know how to value something, the prices will either stay down near zero or will go up near infinity, only eventually settling down to their rightful places when the companies start bringing in earnings and revenues. Now we know for sure that the Internet dream is not a fantasy and we can value Internet companies more accurately.

In the same way, today nobody knows how to value a biotech company. As I write this, both good and bad biotech companies are being valued near zero. But the good ones will break out eventually and will ride parabolic curves toward values near infinity, just as with any bubble that may take years to burst.

So despite my general reservations about stock investing, I invest in companies that diagnose cancer. I invest in companies that I think can diagnose Alzheimer's. I don't like to invest in the cures but I like to invest in the diagnostics. I stay away from the cures because the FDA charges you $2 billion to test your cure and then they still might reject you, which doesn't seem very fair. Given our aging population, the FDA does much more harm than good now. But I do look into more natural causes for curing things. It's important to be aware that the FDA and the pharmaceutical industries have a vested interest in charging some of us tens of thousands a year for a medicine, when we could be seeking more natural cures at a fraction of the cost. So billions have been spent to suppress useful information about many diseases.

I keep track of all of it. It probably would make a good newsletter if someone was so inclined. Now, who might that someone be . . . ?

TREND #2: HEALTHCARE

This is a subtrend of Trend #1 as people age and get sick. But it deserves its own section.

Here's a problem: when I switch from one doctor to another, there's no easy way for the new doctor to access all of my health records. There are technological and regulatory issues.

But some companies out there are figuring out ways to overcome these issues. Software that helps human resources deal with all the new changes in healthcare laws will be a huge trend.

By being on the board of directors of an employment agency with over a billion in revenues, I've become the ultimate HR department. I see the trends that people are innovating in this space. It's an enormous space and the companies that get it right will make billions.

TREND #3 : OBSERVATION

You are being watched. And the people who are watching you are getting better at it. There's direct surveillance and indirect surveillance. When you make a purchase or a phone call, indirect surveillance hones in on certain patterns and either labels you as a terrorist or not. They don't know or ask who you are until they need to.

Direct surveillance involves the satellites that are constantly taking photos of your street and sending them to the government. There are companies that do this. When you surf a website about lingerie and then go to the *New York Times* op-ed website, what do you see? An ad for Victoria's Secret on the right. This is called "retargeting." There are companies that look at what you do and then retarget the ads that follow you around the Internet.

When you walk on a street in New York City there are companies that not only look at you the way a camera would, but also look at what you do and analyze it. If you are carrying a backpack, and then you put the backpack down in the middle of the street and walk away, there's a company that rings a little bell somewhere and police are alerted.

You're being watched all the time. And it's only going to get worse/better, depending on how you view it. Fortunately, there are many ways you can take advantage of this trend: you can write a newsletter about the technologies. You can make your own company involved in the "observation industry" (a term I had never heard until recently but an industry valued at over $100 billion). You can buy one or some of the many stocks that keep getting bigger each year. You can work for one of these technologies. You can be a banker or an investor in these technologies, both in the public and the private space. For each trend I've mentioned I've done deals in the industries and I've invested in the industries, and although I haven't started a company in any of these industries, I've helped the people who have.

TREND #4: THE TEMP WORKFORCE

Despite what a lot of people think, trends are neither inherently good nor bad. They are things that are happening to tens of millions of people. Being aware of them allows us to possibly insert ourselves somewhere in the process and benefit.

One trend that's taking place right now is that many people are getting fired or demoted from middle-management positions and have to find other ways to get work. Sometimes they get fired because companies no longer need them. Sometimes they get fired because they get instantly outsourced to temp employment firms that instantly hire them back to the companies that fired them. Why would companies do this? So they don't have to deal anymore with human resources, healthcare, etc.

There are many opportunities in the tech workforce space, including:

- BUYING UP STOCKS of employment firms that are getting more and more technologically savvy about helping to place employees, deal with healthcare issues, etc.
- GETTING INVOLVED in companies that are being used to rehire the

new temp workforce in ways they've never been hired before.

The mobile application Uber, which I first mentioned in an earlier chapter, is an example of one of these companies. Uber allows you to see what cabs are near you so you can hail one electronically. You press a button and your car shows up. This allows people who are out of work, but who have a nice car, to sign up for Uber and make some money. Uber will slowly become a way for a workforce to connect with the people who need it. It's a logistics and workforce software rather than a car-hailing service. And people are embracing it: Uber gave more car rides in San Francisco in October, 2014 then all cab rides combined. Times three.

AirBnB is another example. This website allows people with extra rooms in their home to post the availability online for people looking in that particular place at that particular time. These extra rooms essentially become hotel rooms for people looking for accommodations (except they're usually a lot cheaper). AirBnB has more rooms available in New York than all the hotels *combined*.

Uber and AirBnB are hard to invest in right now because they are private. But figuring out how to piggyback on, or use, their model—which is becoming widely known as "the sharing economy"—will provide ways for people to make money. In essence, people are taking what they already have—homes, cars, time—and using these assets to create wealth.

Or, we can take it one step back: creating an *information product* that studies this trend and gives suggestions on how to make money is another way to generate income.

TREND #5: ROBOTICS

In 1988 I went to a lecture given by MIT professor Rodney Brooks. I was neck deep in studying the technology behind current-day robotics at the time. He said that robots don't have to start out "smart." They can figure out lots of small things along the way—just like humans, he said. He showed an example of a small robot that would bump into a wall a few times, then realize that a wall was there, and turn around and go a different direction. That robot, more than a quarter century later, is now called the Roomba and vacuums your room. It's also called many other things, in many industries, and has enhanced many technologies. Studying this trend will make you money.

We now fight our wars with robots. We perform surgeries with robots. Robots listen to your phone calls. What do robots need? They are hungry for technology, for more powerful batteries. Every battery uses lithium. We're going to go through a worldwide lithium shortage (is this a trend, or a subtrend? I don't know, but it's there). They are going to use more powerful cameras. They are going to use more powerful sensors. They are going to use more powerful techniques to communicate and then store what they learn. What they need changes every day because they are getting more and more powerful.

TREND #6: CHEMISTRY

Alcoa has made aluminum the same way since the late 19th century. Their profits are razor thin because everyone knows the aluminum manufacturing process and anyone can supply the appropriate chemicals and metals at just the right price.

However, this is going to change and someone is going to find a new way to make aluminum. They might discover new elements to use and new processes to smelt. Companies that hoard those elements or develop those new processes will benefit in a big way. Chemistry is going to be much more influential in the coming ten to twenty years than information technology.

Keep track of the changes in how people are innovating in chemistry and suddenly you will see what's happening in alternative energy, battery storage, isolation of valuable chemical isotopes (like pure oxygen, for instance), etc. How do you make money on this? Read about it, keep an eye on the companies and markets involved, and you will see the right moment to place your bets. Just like the biotech markets, the chemistry space is difficult to value but the markets are huge, even in the trillions.

I could've called this trend "alternative energy" but that would be weak. Alternative energy comes and goes. First there's solar, then there's wind, then we're back to solar, and so on. But every change that finds its way back into alternative energy stocks starts off in a chemistry lab. I like to be where the technology is happening, as close to the laboratory as possible, in order to understand where to invest or where to build. Does this mean I need to be a chemist? Not at all. I barely know what the periodic table is. But I am able to read the latest reports and try to figure out how they are going to be applied. Understanding trends is not a day trader's game. It's the long game. But since trends are so hard to value at the beginning, there are enormous profits to be made.

TREND #7: FINANCIAL TECHNOLOGY

When I did my podcast with entrepreneur and venture capitalist Peter Thiel, he was an hour late. This wasn't a problem. He let me know he was running late. It actually made the podcast more interesting to me, because it gave me the perfect starting question: What were you doing during the past hour? Thiel's answer: "We were looking at new innovations in financial technology."

There are many things happening in the financial technology world. For starters, the rise of the cashless economy. What Thiel started when he cofounded PayPal is ongoing. Can I go to a hotel, pick up my key at a kiosk, go to my room, stay overnight, and then walk out, without having to pay or deal with a line and tips and a desk clerk and so on? Yes, I can. And this is only one example of the sort of thing that will begin to happen in every service industry.

The global economy has always been subject to policies that are restrictive of money exchange. Let's say I buy an item from you and you are in China (something that can easily happen in a global economy). I have to send you a wire. This can turn into a huge hassle. First there are fees at my bank. Then there are fees at the local Federal Reserve. Then there are fees at your country's central bank. Then there are international wire fees. Then there are fees down the chain at the central bank in China and the local bank there. Not to mention the taxes every step of the way. What do all of these fees add up to? Inflation. The global economy creates layers and layers of fees that are hidden inside almost every transaction that you make now.

Of course, this was the old way. Fortunately for us, there are now forces at work to eliminate that. The software-based online payment system bitcoin is one such force.

I don't know whether bitcoin will work or if people will embrace this form of money exchange. But I keep track of it and I keep track of the companies that are innovating on top of it. I even released *Choose Yourself!* a month early last year as a bitcoin-only book.

Someone wrote an article saying that *Choose Yourself!* was the best-selling book ever on bitcoin. CNBC had me on and asked, "Did you just do this as a marketing gimmick?" and I said, "Well, I'm on national TV right now, aren't I?" Guess what domain name belonged to most of the people who bought the book using bitcoin: amazon.com. So whether or not bitcoin is the winner, I have no idea. But someone will win, and many people are looking at ways to do this.

Payday loans are another phenomenon in financial technology. There's a massive alternative banking industry comprised of people who, for various reasons, don't use traditional banks. I'm not sure why they've opted to do this. Maybe they don't trust the banks or maybe the banks don't trust them.

But here's something that will never go away: people who live paycheck to paycheck, a rising phenomenon, often need money the day or days before their check arrives. What do they do? They go to a payday loan company that might charge them one dollar for a hundred-dollar check even though their paycheck may be there tomorrow. That's 365 percent interest. A payday lender charges much higher interest rates than the banks. Sometimes this is regulated, sometimes it isn't. It's a great business to be in but there's one problem. Many people who borrow money are scamming the lender. There's no check coming. This is not a frequent problem but it's a problem in the industry and keeps margins low.

What if *you* can solve this problem? For instance, PayPal used to use software to identify which potential customers were engaging in fraudulent transactions. Once they built this software, their margins went way up. I have no idea what Peter Thiel was talking about the day of the podcast when he said he'd been "looking at innovations in financial technology," but perhaps this was kind of software was one idea. Keeping track of the changes in this space will make readers a lot of money.

CONCLUSION

T he purpose of this chapter on trends is not to predict the future. Nobody can do that. It's like when Swine Flu killed one person and then the UN announced that 200 million people around the world will die of Swine Flu in 2008. Nobody died of Swine Flu in 2008. But there was a stock with the symbol HOGS that fell 20% that day. That's an opportunity to buy. Because most predictions are wrong, so many irrational things happen when a trusted source makes an outrageous prediction.

And there are trends that are irrefutable:
- People are getting older
- The nature of the workforce is changing
- People want alternative energy
- The economy is getting more globalized.
- Robotics is being used for more functions.
- Wearable computing is generating larger and larger revenues.

Think of each trend like a rainstorm. It's coming down and you can't block it. But you can open up an umbrella and be safe. There are many things that can fit under a big umbrella. The bigger the trend, the bigger the umbrella you can have. Thinking of each trend and the things that fit under those umbrellas: stocks, new businesses, new information products, new ways to live your life, is going to be an important part of how to live a "Choose Yourself" lifestyle. What's been happening since "Choose Yourself" came out is that people are forming meetups in their cities to discuss not only how they are making use of the "Daily Practice" that lays the foundation of how to live a healthy *Choose Yourself* lifestyle, but also to share their thoughts and entrepreneurial ideas around these trends, and money is being made.

I discuss how to operate a *Choose Yourself* meetup in a later chapter and I'll set up ways online at jamesaltucher.com so people can share more about their meetups but I'm not involved at all in them. It's just like-minded people getting together to help each other improve their lives. We can feed ourselves but ultimately life is better when we feed each other. It's my hope that the purpose of this chapter and others will point people in a better direction to live their lives.

I've made use of each one of the above trends to make my life better. For instance, when I saw the trend in employment, I went on the board of an employment agency, they've been implementing my ideas, and everyone makes money. When I saw the trend and people getting older, I started investing in startups that diagnose cancer and some of these startups have now gone public. Once you build the foundation of the Daily Practice, then develop the skills and habits described in this book, and then build or participate in a community of like-minded people, you will also be able to benefit from the trends that are affecting your and everyone else's lives.

LESSONS I LEARNED FROM BUILDING A BUSINESS

Back in late 2006, I had to shut down my fund. People who had invested in me—who trusted me to, in turn, invest in what I thought were the best hedge funds—were furious at me. I had been analyzing probably close to a thousand funds to find what I felt were the best ones. I had been up almost every month for my investors. I was doing a decent job raising money. I had a business.

But I couldn't sleep at night, because I couldn't understand how my funds were making money. When I can't understand something and nobody can explain it to me, then I have nightmares—particularly when a lot of money is on the line. So I pulled about $70 million out of the funds I was invested in and returned it to my investors. They were very upset even though they had all made money. None of them wanted me to take fees while I was winding down the fund.

In every business I had ever started, even ones that had totally failed, I had kept good relations with the investors. Except for this one. Not a single relationship survived, even though I had made money for everyone. When things are confusing, when you can't understand how or why or whether or not you *should* be making money, it's time to switch focus. In 1998 when kids in high school were learning how to make websites, I sold my website design business for $15 million. Two years later almost all website design businesses were out of business.

So now, in 2006, no matter how hard I tried to figure it out, it seemed like the world economy had gone crazy. I needed something to do or I would quickly go broke. I sort of just shut the fund down without thinking of the consequences and *then* I realized I was going to go broke. *Again.*

Here's exactly what I did then:

I spec'd out a website I wanted to make: a financial site that had no news on it but was focused on building community by exchanging ideas. When I say, "spec'd," I mean I wrote down what all the buttons on the front page would do and what other content would appear on the front page. I completely defined the next five layers of the site and what buttons and actions and content would occur on each page.

Once I had the specs, I went to a firm in India and asked them to design five pages of the website. Just the design. No code. This cost me five hundred dollars I showed those pages to a potential distribution partner (thestreet.com) and worked out a deal where they would help me get traffic and would place ads in exchange for 50 percent ownership. They had a billion page views a year, so I said, "*Yes!*" (Actually, that's not quite true. I said, I was thinking 3 percent ownership for them, and they said, "No, 50 percent," and then I said, "*Yes!*")

I paid the Indian firm to finish the site, which cost $2,000. Then I came up with more ideas for the site and more ideas and more ideas, and although we did a soft launch at version 1.0, we did a hard launch at version 5.0 about five months later.

I got my friends to use the site. For a while, I created over seven hundred fake users and manually entered in probably over 10,000 pieces of data onto the site just to make it useful right away. This taught me an important lesson that I now pass along to you: don't be afraid to do things manually to get things going on your site. Even with user-generated content, it's OK if you are the first thousand users if you expect a million users to benefit from it.

I got my friends to write reviews of the site on their popular blogs. I wrote articles that would link back to the useful content on the site. I guest blogged on many different websites. This is how you get users back to your site. It's true for any site: financial sites, bird-watching sites, weight loss sites, sports sites, whatever.

I created three areas of community on the site: a way for people to message and have "friends," a user-generated forum system, and a Q&A system. The Q&A system in particular generated 40 percent of the traffic the day after it launched. At this point, I had ads on every page, a million users a month...and no employees. So we were profitable. We were making about $100,000 in just four months. But because I was too afraid to build this into a big business, I sold the site almost instantly.

I could've used other examples. I could've used the debit card business I started. The delivery service I started. The mental health hospital I was involved in. The billion-revenues business I'm on the board of directors of, and the many other businesses I've advised and consulted with and invested in. But the lessons I've learned are all the same. There are things you *have* to do when you start a company, no matter what kind of company it is.

❦

Get Down on Your Hands and Knees and Scrub

Even when something is scalable, don't be afraid to get down on your hands and knees and be the first part of that scaling. Don't expect anonymous users or computers to do all your initial hard work. No one cares about this venture like *you* do. You do all your initial hard work.

❦

Provide Free Content on The Front Page

I had so much free content available it almost obscured the design. But I wasn't a graphic artist. I was mostly concerned about getting people as much quality information as possible as quickly as possible, so they would then sign up for the site's more advanced features. Once I had an e-mail address I had more opportunities to market to them. Give away as much for free as possible so you can get that e-mail address.

❦

Outsource in Incremental Stages

First we designed pages, and then after we knew we were going to get big distribution, we made the rest of the site. Then, based on user feedback and more ideas, we designed four more versions before an official launch. The site changed drastically from version 1.0 to version 5.0. You save a lot of time and money when you can learn as you go and use what you know to make better decisions for your growing business. Remember what I said about to-do lists? They never work because you really don't know what should go on them when you start a project. The same goes for your business.

⁓

Diversify Your Distribution

Although there was one primary source of distribution (thestreet.com) from which I was getting traffic, I also worked out deals to get traffic from AOL, Yahoo, *Forbes*, Reuters, and basic advertising. I would post articles there and link back to my site.

Ultimately I had traffic coming from about 20 different websites. Never let one company decide your fate. 1000s of businesses have been lost because of this one mistake.

⁓

Don't Spend Time Worrying About Competition

Here's how: I had competition but they were using the "build it and they will come" technique. Ninety-five percent of businesses forget that it's important for you to be the first heavy users of your product (back to the first point I made).

I'll be honest: when I first realized I had competition, I cried. I actually called the developers in India and told them it was all over. They had to cheer me up. One thing I ultimately learned was that the biggest asset the business had was the passion my partner and I had for it. That passion was much higher than the passion of our competitors, so we ended up creating and implementing the best ideas. End of competition.

A restaurant is a great example of this. Its initial success doesn't depend just on how good the food is, but how many of your friends and their friends come in the door to buy it. Don't be afraid to call everyone in your Rolodex to come on over and try the food.

∽

It Doesn't Matter if You Know Anyone

I certainly didn't. I cold-called Yahoo, AOL, and *Forbes* to get on their radar. In fact, I had a "negative network." The first guy I called at Yahoo said he knew me. "Oh yeah?" I said because I had no idea who he was.

He said, "Yeah, I invested in your wireless Internet business and lost my investment."

You would think that would have hurt my chances. But Yahoo became one of my biggest sources of distribution after that call. And that guy became my biggest advocate within Yahoo.

The key is to anticipate what the people you're aiming to serve might want, show them how it will cost them nothing but they will get huge benefit from it, and then just simply do it. Make it as easy as possible for the other side to say yes before you ask them.

If you want someone to say yes, show them exactly what "yes" looks like and show them that it is already made.

∽

Combine Interests

I had already spent twenty years in the technology business (since the time I was in college). And I had been in the financial industry for about seven years. So

I combined interests and made the best financial website. Nobody else was as well placed in this intersection as I was.

Maybe there isn't one thing you do better than anyone else. But I bet there are two things you're pretty good at that haven't been combined before. *Poof!* You're the one to do it.

✑

MAKE IT A BUSINESS YOU WOULD USE

In the financial industry I was a writer, a day trader, and a hedge fund manager, and I was probably an expert in all three areas. Expert enough to write five books on the topic. Which, of course, means nothing but I'm going to say it anyway.

So when I set out to make a website I created the website I *would use.* One with no news, but tons of interesting ideas, perspectives, and community. Reading news never made anyone rich, but it is very common in the hedge fund business for professional investors to call one another and exchange ideas. Hedge fund managers are on the phone all day with one another. I made it very simple for everyone, and not just hedge fund managers, to do that online.

✑

ABD—ALWAYS BE DEAL MAKING

Even though I had a 50 percent distribution partner right from the beginning, I was constantly meeting with companies and people to see what extra deals I could make.

I would come up with ideas about the value I could deliver them and then I would offer up that value. Maybe they needed a white label version of my site. Maybe they needed content from my site. Maybe they needed their blog to be distributed on my site, or maybe they wanted their newsletter sold on my site. I did any deal I could do. Until finally I sold the site. But that wasn't even the final deal. I stuck with it and the site continued to grow.

Realize That Nothing is a Straight Line

There were constant cases where the code was bad on the site and times when it would crash if it had too many users at the same time. I thought I was going to have a heart attack every other week because the site kept crashing.

And some companies were very slow to do deals with me. Some companies outright rejected me (Google). You can't be bitter or burn bridges. There may come another day, another company, or all the people at Google might move to other places where you do business. The key here is to always stay in touch and provide monthly updates showing how you are improving things. Always be willing to help people no matter what. Things don't move in a linear way. There are ups and downs and good days and bad days, as with anything else in life.

Realize That You'll Know When to Give Up if The Time Ever Comes

I was willing to give up every step of the way if I didn't see some form of traction. Sometimes that meant more users. Sometimes that meant more profits. Sometimes that meant more reviews. Sometimes, I don't know, I just got more excited.

Build Community By Hand and In Person

I traveled around the country holding meet-ups with the most active users so I could see with my own eyes how the site was helping people. It was exciting to me. As long as I had that excitement, I knew something was working.

168

Why did I go myself to most of these meet-ups? There's a saying in Argentina, "When the CEO is looking, the cow grows fatter." A business builds fastest when the CEO is looking at it, because he or she sees a thousand details. The COO sees a hundred details, the regular employee ten. And details slip through the cracks when there is nobody looking.

Perseverance is like a fire that needs oxygen. Love is the oxygen for perseverance. You can love it. Users can love it. Partners can love it. Investors can love it. There are a lot of sources of love.

Ultimately, you create value for people and that's how you build the love. Think of your business as the delivery mechanism of that love.

Then, love + perseverance = abundance.

And if you want the world to get better, you write about that love and abundance and share it with others.

A Cheat-Sheet for Starting and Building a Business

This chapter includes the nuts and bolts, an FAQ on starting a business. If you're a lawyer, feel free to disagree with me so you can charge someone your BS fees to give the same advice. If you can think of anything to add, please go to AskAltucher.com and tell me. I might be missing things. If you want to argue with me, feel free. I might be wrong on any of the items below.

There are many types of business. Depending on your business, some of these questions won't apply. All of them come from questions I've been asked.

The rules are: I'm not always going to give explanations. Just read.

C Corp or S Corp or LLC? C Corp.

- *What state should I incorporate in?* Delaware.
- *Should founders vest?* Yes, over a period of four years. The vesting speeds up on any change of control.
- *Should I go for venture capital money?* First build a product, then get a customer, then get friends and family money (or money from revenues, which is cheapest of all) and then think about raising money. But only then.
- *Should I patent my idea?* Get customers first. Patent later. Don't talk to lawyers until the last possible moment.
- *Should I require venture capitalists to sign NDAs?* No. Nobody is going to steal your idea.
- *How much equity should I give a partner?* Divide things up in equal portions into these categories: manages the company, raises the money, had the idea, brings in the revenues, built the product (or performs the services).

- *Should I have a technical cofounder if I'm not technical?* No. If you don't already have a technical cofounder you can always outsource technology and not give up equity.
- *Should I barter equity for services?* No. You get what you pay for.
- *How do I market my app?* Friends, and then word of mouth.
- *Should I build a product?* Maybe. But first manually see if your product works. Then think about providing it as a service. Then productize the commonly used services. Too many people do this in reverse and then fail.
- *How much dilution is too much dilution?* If someone wants to give you money, then take it. The old saying, 100 percent of nothing is worth less than one percent of something.
- *Should I listen to venture capitalists?* Yes, of course. They gave you money. But then don't do anything they ask you to do.
- *What if nobody seems to be buying my product?* Then change to a service and do whatever anyone is willing to pay for.
- *If a client wants me to hire their friend or they won't give me the business (i.e., like a bribe). What should I do?* Always do the ethical thing—hire the friend and get the client's business.
- *What do I do when a customer rejects me in a B2B business?* Stay in touch once a month. Never be angry.
- *In a B2C business:* release fast. Add new features every week.
- *How do I get new clients?* The best new clients are old clients. Always offer new services.
- *What if my client asks you to do something not in your business plan?* Do it, or find someone who can do it, even if it's a competitor.
- *Should I ever focus on SEO?* No.
- *Should I do social media marketing?* No.
- *Should I ever talk badly about a partner of an employee even though they are awful?* Never gossip. Always be straight with the culprit.
- *I have lots of ideas. How do I pick the right one?* Execute on as many as pos-

sible. The right idea will pick you.

- *What are some telltale signs of an amateur businessperson?* Doing any of these things:
  - Having fights with partners in the first year. Fire them or split before anything gets out of control.
  - Worrying about dilution.
  - Trying to get Mark Cuban to invest because "this would be great for the Dallas Mavericks."
  - Asking people you barely know to introduce you to Mark Cuban.
  - Asking people for five minutes of their time. It's never five minutes so you are establishing yourself as a liar.
  - Having a PowerPoint that doesn't show me arbitrage. I need to know that there is a small chance I'll see a hundred-fold return on my money.
  - Catch-22: showing people there are a small chance they'll see a hundred-fold return on their money. The secret of salesmanship is getting through the Catch-22.
  - Rejecting a cash offer for your company when you have almost no revenues. Hello Friendster and foursquare.

- *What are some signs of a professional?*
  - Going from bullshit product to services to software as a service (SaaS) product. (Corollary: the reverse is amateur hour).
  - Cutting costs every day.
  - When you have a billion in revenues, staying focused. When you have zero revenues, staying unfocused and coming up with new ideas every day.
  - Saying no to people who are obvious losers.
  - Saying yes to any meeting at all with someone who is an obvious winner.
  - Knowing how to distinguish between winners and losers (you know in your gut, trust me).

- *When should I hire people full-time?* When you have revenues
- *How long does it take to raise money?* In a great business, six months. In a mediocre business: infinity.
- *Should I get an office?* Not unless you have revenues.
- *Should I do market research?* Yes, find one customer who definitely, without a doubt, will buy a service from you. Note, I don't say buy your product because your initial product is always not what the customer wanted.
- *Should I pay taxes?* No. You should always reinvest your money and operate at a loss.
- *Should I pay dividends?* See above.
- *What should the CEO salary be?* No more than two times that of your lowest employee if you are not profitable. This even assumes you are funded. If you are not funded your salary should be zero until your revenues can pay your salary last. The CEO salary is the last expense paid in every business.
- *When should I fire employees?* When you have less than six months burn in the bank and revenues aren't growing fast enough.
- *When should one have sex with an employee?* When you love her and the feeling is mutual.
- *When should one fire an employee?* When they gossip. When they don't over-deliver constantly. When they ask for a raise because they think they are making below industry standard. When the talk badly about a client. When they have an attitude.
- *When should you give a raise?* Rarely.
- *How big should the employee option pool be?* Fifteen to 20 percent.
- *How much do advisers get?* One-quarter of one percent. Advisers are useless. Don't even have an advisory board.
- *How much do board members get?* Nothing. They should all be investors. If they aren't an investor, then one-half of one percent
- *Should you take the offer to buy your company?* Yes. In cash.

- *What is the only effective e-mail marketing?* Highly targeted e-mail marketing written by professional copywriters and the e-mail list is made up of people who have bought similar services in the past six months. Corollary: If you have zero skills as a copywriter, then everything you write will be boring.

- *Should I give stuff for free?* Maybe. But don't expect free customers to turn into paying customers. Your free customers actually hate you and want everything from you for nothing so you better have a different business model.

- *Should I have schwag?* No.

- *Should I go to SXSW?* No.

- *Should I go to industry parties and meet-ups?* No.

- *Should I blog?* Yes. You must. Blog about everything going wrong in your industry. Blog personal stories that you think will scare away customers. They won't. Customers will be attracted to your honesty.

- *Should I care about margins?* No. Care about revenues.

- *Should I spin off this unrelated idea into a separate business?* No. Make one business great. Throw everything into it. Do DBA (a legal term for "doing business as") to identify different ideas.

- *Should I hire people because I can travel on a seven-hour plane ride with them?* Don't be an idiot. If anything, hire people who are the opposite of you. Otherwise, who will you delegate to?

- *When should I say no to a client?* When they initially approach you.

- *When should I say yes to a client?* Every other conversation you ever have with them after that initial no.

- *Should I have sex with an employee?* Stop asking that.

- *Should I negotiate the best terms with a VC?* No. Pick the VC you like. Times are going to get tough at some point and you'll need to be able to have a heart to heart with them.

- *Should I give employees bonuses for a job well done?* No. Give them gifts but not bonuses.

- *What should I do at Christmas?* Send everyone you know a gift basket.

- *When should I give up on my idea?* When you can't generate revenues, customers, interest, for two months.
- *Why didn't the VC or customer call back after we met yesterday and it was great?* Because they hate you.
- *Why didn't the above call back after we met yesterday and it was great?* "Yesterday" was like a split second ago for them and a lifetime for you. There's the law of entrepreneurial relativity. Figure out what that means and live by it.
- *Should I hire a professional CEO?* No. Never.
- *Should I hire a head of sales?* No. The founder is the head of sales until at least $10 million in sales.
- *My client called at 3 a.m. Should I tell him to respect boundaries?* No. You no longer have any boundaries.
- *I made a mistake. Should I tell the client?* Yes. Tell him everything that happened. You're his partner. Not the guy that hides things and then lies about them.
- *My investors want me to focus on one thing. Should I listen to them?* No. Diversify in every way you can.
- *I personally need money. Should I borrow from the business?* Only if the business can survive for another six months no matter what happens.
- *I just bought two companies. Should I put them under the same roof and start consolidating?* No. Not for at least two years.
- *Should I quit my job?* No. Only if you have salary that can pay you for six months at your start-up. Aim to quit your job but don't actually quit your job.
- *What do I do when I have doubts?* Ask your customers if your doubts are trustworthy.
- *I have too much competition. What should I do?* Competition is good. It shows you have a decent business model. Now simply outperform them.
- *My wife/husband thinks I spend too much time on my start-up. What do I do?* Divorce them or stop your business.
- *I'm starting my business but I have relationship problems. What should I do?*

175

Get rid of your relationship.

- *Should I expand geographically as quickly as possible?* No. Get all the business you can in your local area. Travel takes up too much time.

- *I undercharged. What should I do about it?* Nothing, now. Charge the next client more.

- *I have an idea for an app but don't know how to execute. What should I do?* Draw every screen and function. Then outsource someone to make the drawings look like they come from a real app. Then outsource the development of the app. Get a specific schedule. Micromanage the schedule.

- *I want to buy a franchise in X. Is that a good idea?* Only buy a franchise if it's underperforming and you can figure out how to improve it. Don't buy on future hopes, only on past mistakes.

- *I want to buy a business in X. Is that a good idea?* Rely on the three D's: Death, Debt, Divorce. When someone dies, the heirs will sell a business cheap. When someone is in debt, they will sell a business cheap. When someone divorces, the couple usually has to sell a business cheap. Important: even if the industry trends are in your favor, you cannot predict the future. But you can use the past to help you get a deal. Always get a deal.

- *I have a lot of website traffic but no revenues. What should I do?* Sell your business. There's only one Google. (Well, there's two or three Googles, if you count Facebook and Twitter. But you're not any of them).

- *I have no traffic. How do I get traffic?* Shut down your business.

- *Should I hire a PR firm?* No. Do guerilla marketing. Read Newsjacking and *Trust Me, I'm Lying.* PR firms screw up from beginning to the end. The first time I hired a PR firm, instead of sending me my contract they accidentally sent me their contract for Terry Bradshaw. He was paying $12,000 a month. Was it worth it for him?

- *My competition is doing better than me across every metric. What should I do?* Don't be afraid to instantly shut down your business and start over if you can't sell the business. Time is a horrible thing to waste.

- *I have been in business now for six years and my business doesn't seem to be growing. It's even slowing down. What should I do?* Come up with ten ideas a day about new services your business can offer. Try to get a customer for each new service. I know one business in this situation that refuses to do this because their VCs are telling them to focus more. You're going to go out of business otherwise.

- *Is it unethical to run my business from the side while still at my job?* I don't know. Did God tell you that in a dream?

- *My customer called me at 5 p.m. on a Friday and said, "We have to talk" and now I can't talk to him until Monday. What does it mean?* It means you're fired.

- *XYZ just sold for a $100 million. Should I be valued at that?* I'm better! No, you should shut up.

- *Investors want to meet me and customers want to meet me. Who do I meet if I need money?* You should know the answer to that by now.

- *If an acquirer asks me why I want to sell, what should I say?* That you feel it would be easier for you to grow in the context of a bigger company that has experienced the growing pains you are just starting to go through.

- *I just started my business. What should I do?* Sell it as fast as possible (applies in 99 percent of situations).

- *If you're so smart why aren't you a billionaire?* Because I sold my businesses early, lost everything, started new businesses, sold them, and got lucky every now and then.

- *Should I even start a business?* No. Make money. Build stuff. Then start a business.

Why I Want My Kids to Know Who the Mysterious S. J. Scott Is

Whenever I write something like "Quit your job!" or "Don't go to college!" there are always people who comment, "Not everyone can be an entrepreneur!" People get very angry. Like somehow I'm suggesting people stop reading Chaucer and make solar cars instead.

The thing is, these people are right. They probably *can't* be entrepreneurs if they are so insistent that they can't. Nobody has a gun to their head to make the next Google. But they also are misreading my words, which is probably my fault. I'm not giving advice. I'm merely saying what the reality is, and I'll say it again: the age of domesticated cubicle jobs, an era that lasted only about one hundred years out of the past 4 million, is over. People are getting fired. That way of life is over. Everyone is getting outsourced or replaced by robots or just downsized or demoted. That world is depressing and oppressing if you are trying to cling to the past and keep climbing that ladder, since everything you cling to will ultimately disappoint you.

And college . . . that's over also.

There's a guy out there named Steve Scott—the mysterious Steve Scott, aka S. J. Scott, maybe aka other names I don't even know. His books kept popping up everywhere—often beating my books on the various Amazon lists. How could *23 Anti-Procrastination Habits* rank higher than *Choose Yourself!*? Who the hell is this guy, I wondered? And he was writing other books, too, with titles like *70 Healthy Habits*, or *How to Start a Successful Blog in One Hour*. And every few weeks there would be another book.

At first I noticed the books appear under the name Steve Scott. But then, with a completely different picture of the author, I noticed the same kind of books coming up under "S. J. Scott." He was like a machine for books: *Is $.99 the New Free? Declutter Your Inbox*, and on and on.

So I finally called him. I didn't know him. I didn't have any friends who knew him. I think he lives in the middle of Ohio. But I wanted to know what the hell he was doing. I wanted my kids to do it so they would never have to have the worries and anxieties that I had all through my twenties and thirties. He told me just two years ago he was dead broke and trying to figure out what to do. He had basically zero in the bank and was making no money.

"Last month I made over $40,000," he told me. He's written forty-two books in the past two years. He now writes a book every three weeks.

"Can anyone do this?" I asked him.

"Yes," he said, and we made a podcast out of it because I wanted everyone to hear his detailed answers.

Scott basically writes 2,000 words a day. In the front of each book he has various things he gives away for free if people sign up for his e-mail list.

"Take a concept you're interested in," he told me, "and break it up into a lot of parts and write a book about each part.

"For instance, if you are interested in golf, write a book about how to get the right equipment, write a book about how to improve your swing in ten easy steps, write a book, *Learn to Putt 100 Percent Better in Sixty Minutes*, and so on."

Each book gets him more e-mail subscribers. More e-mail subscribers gets him more book sales. And so on. Did he study writing or marketing in college? You decide: he majored in criminal psychology at Montclair State University. It took two years to build up but now he is a marketing and entrepreneurial machine even though he has never done anything like this before. He has no boss. He enjoys his free time. He makes more money than 95 percent of the CEOs in the corporate world.

I asked him why he was being so transparent. Why he was telling me *every-thing*. "Can't anyone just copy what you do?"

"Sure," he says. "But I work really hard."

COMPOUND INTEREST AND COMPOUND ABUNDANCE

Albert Einstein supposedly said, "The eighth wonder of the world is compound interest." The idea that if you put some money in the bank and let it sit there or invest it wisely it will somehow allow it to "compound" into millions of dollars by the time you need it does sound somewhat wondrous. This quote has been the underpinnings of many books, shows, marketing campaigns, and myths about personal finance. Too bad it's total nonsense—and a myth that's cost people millions of dollars.

First off, Einstein never said it. In 1983 the *New York Times* claimed that he did, but nowhere else before that (and he died in 1955) is there evidence he said it.

However, Johnny Carson said something about compound interest on *The Tonight Show* in the early '80s that is very real and very true: "Scientists have developed a powerful new weapon that destroys people but leaves buildings standing—it's called the 17 percent interest rate." In other words, saving money is all fine and good. But when inflation hits, and financial meltdowns happen and you're in debt, chances are your money hasn't compounded enough to help you when you most need the money.

There are stories about some janitor who dies and it turns out he had $90 million saved up because he invested in Exxon in 1950 and he reinvested the dividends, etc. Maybe one or two of those stories are true, but that is not the norm. Those are anecdotes used in commercials by people who want to capture your fees to build their business.

First off, inflation is always going to rise faster than the value of money left in a savings account. There's rarely been a period where that didn't happen (the Great Depression and early 2009 are the only examples I can think of).

Second, nobody can merely *invest* their way to wealth, not even Warren

Buffett. Warren Buffett made fees on his hedge funds and reinvested those. That is how he made the initial part of his wealth. Then he used the money people put into his insurance companies, invested that, and kept 100 percent of the profits, and that's how he made billions. So compounding, by itself, will never make you rich. The argument for saving money is that it then begins to work for you. But there are much better ways for your money to work for you than compound interest, which is the fool's gold found at the end of a rainbow. You can chase after it but you'll never find it.

The word *interest* usually refers to money. Since we know money is a side effect of abundance I try to think of this in a different way.

When I start to date a woman, I want her to love me *immediately.* Of course, that never happens. "You're going too fast," she says, and she ends it. When I started a novel when I was younger, I wanted to finish it the next day. When I start a business, I want to sell it a day later and count my riches. When I started graduate school, I was already planning how I was going to be the fastest PhD in history. Around the time that I had initially planned on receiving that PhD, I ended up getting thrown out for "lack of maturity," according to the letter I received.

I don't believe the claim that life is short. Sometimes it feels very long. Like I wish every day would be over already just so I can get to the next. And the next. An imaginary tomorrow always seems to be better than today in my head. Which makes me think of my hero, Gene Wolfe. Gene Wolfe understood the principles of compound abundance.

And he displayed that knowledge by giving us Pringles.

Gene Wolfe was given the task of taking a baked potato, pressing it down, and slicing it up in such a way that it would fit into a tennis ball can. And he did it. He invented Pringles. And I ate one this morning. But that's not why he's my hero. While many normal human beings, not as obsessed with status and creativity as Gene was, might say: "OK, I just did my life's achievement. I've achieved my *purpose.* I've created an easily storable food based on a vegetable that, when doused with a ton of salt, will please children and adults for decades, maybe centuries." I mean, what would you do at that point? If I were Gene (and I almost hate using his first name, as if I know him when it's only in my dreams that I imagine having dinner with him and, *oh,* the things we would talk about, the laughs we would have) I would've rested on my laurels, collected awards, imagined playing golf with friends, can of Pringles always in tow, maybe a little belly develops, but, hey, he deserved it. He *earned* it.

But Gene knew the magic secret. And it is only with the record of his lifetime (and at eighty-three he's still going) that he is able to share that secret.

THE SECRET: ONE PAGE A DAY.

Gene has been an adult for almost 25,000 days. He writes a page a day. A page is about three hundred words words. A paragraph or two. Can you do that? Twenty-five thousand pages. About eighty books' worth of pages. Gene ended up writing fifty published novels, including many best-sellers and award winners. He didn't get stereotyped and stuffed into that Pringles can, as dead as the chips he created. He did what he loved to do. That's what keeps you alive every day. That's the Push. Life is too long to reject the opportunities in front of you every day.

I was talking to James Manos, the creator of the HBO hit show *Dexter.* He said, "My definition of success is if you can't distinguish between work and pleasure."

It's OK if right now the two are separate for you. Today is a new day.

We repent what we want to change. We regret what we never changed.

Today I wrote this page.

Value Your Business the "Choose Yourself" Way: The Secret of Abundance

A friend of mine bought a chain of about thirty pizza stores that were "underperforming." They were in great locations: all near college campuses. And they all had a great brand name, which you likely know: Domino's. My friend had been a high-up executive at Domino's but now he wanted to branch out on his own, so he bought the thirty Domino's stores and "turned them around." He then sold them and became very wealthy. I asked him: "How hard could it be to turn around a Domino's store?" He said, "It's very simple. Make round pizzas."

Apparently the Domino's that he took over were poorly managed, and the pizzas weren't coming out consistent. They were odd-shaped, which was ruining the brand. Additionally, they would claim the pizza would arrive in thirty minutes when in reality it would arrive in forty-five—also inconsistent with the brand. An important part of the Domino's brand is that it's not a location restaurant. It's a delivery service. If you are known as a quality delivery service, you better deliver when you say you are.

So because these locations were struggling, my friend was able to buy them cheap. He then determined *why* they were struggling, and fixed those two items: make round pizzas and deliver on time. And then he became an enormous success. He didn't need to discover the next Facebook to be a success. He just understood the basics of business and was able, fairly quickly, to make *extremely simple* adjustments, and because of that he made millions.

There are a lot of points to address here.

First off, I should mention that Ray Kroc was fifty-nine years old when he bought the McDonald's franchise. Just a few years earlier he had been working paycheck to paycheck to pay for the rent on his one-room apartment. This is just another example of how it's *never too late* to choose yourself.

Was serving clean food Ray's dream or passion? Of course not. After he retired, at the age of seventy-three, he bought the San Diego Padres. My guess is that was closer to his favorite passions. Passions he had discovered within himself when he was just a little boy. Sometimes it takes a while to get to do what we love, but it's always worth it.

Second, it costs money to buy a franchise or buy McDonald's or whatever.

Or does it?

The company that once owned the thirty Domino's franchises mentioned above was going out of business. If a company has no or declining cash flow, debt, employees to pay, and is about to go out of business, then what is it worth? Well, it depends on the negotiation. This is a very important point about business.

We know, thanks to the Idea Matrix presented earlier in this book, that ideas are more valuable than money. The man with more ideas will be able to out negotiate the man with fewer ideas. The man with fewer ideas might say to himself: "I'm about to go out of business and I will be broke and I have no idea how to improve this business and here is a nice man willing to actually give me cold hard cash for this useless business." The man with ideas might be able to say: "Round pizzas = instant turnaround = huge cash flows of millions of dollars." Both are looking at the same thing.

People claim that they can value a business by looking at their profit statements. Nothing can be further from the truth. These traditional, or old school, businessmen will soon find themselves out of business. This is the old way of looking at things. The new rules require us to recognize that ideas as currency become critical when both sides of a negotiation are looking at the same thing. The person with more ideas doesn't need to negotiate hard. There are no secret tricks, although he'd be wise to follow the tips given in the earlier chapter on negotiation. It's just a matter of identifying what the value is in the other side's eyes and meeting that value. Remember: good negotiations are win-win. Both sides get what they want.

Let's say that in the Domino's case the selling location owners were so afraid it was worth zero that they were willing to take anything but they put up a confident front. Maybe they said, "$100,000" per store. My friend saw millions in potential per store so this might not have hurt him. But that's a lot of money, you might say! $3 million!

184

Again, ideas are more valuable than money. Ideas are currency. Money itself is meaningless. It's just pieces of paper that our minds have assigned value to.

If you are twenty-two-years old you might not be able to get the $3 million. You might not yet have enough friends, family, network, experience, to command the trust in your ideas that an older person can command. Or you might. I don't know. But basically, raising money is a matter of presenting ideas. How do you raise $3 million? In this case:

- You say *who* you are. My friend had been in the pizza business for a while, but as an employee and not an owner.
- You say *why* you can run these locations.
- You say *how* you are going to turn them around and you get specific (round pizzas, consistent delivery times).
- Most importantly, you *be specific:* Exactly how are you going to make round-er pizzas and better delivery times? This is just a matter of keeping an eye on the business and hiring the right employees.

Many owners get bored of their businesses, or are not qualified to run them. There are reasons for this that we'll discuss in a second.

There's the Argentinean motto I cited in an earlier chapter: "When the CEO is looking, the cow grows fatter." If you have ever been to Argentina, you know that the one true religion there is steak. They have their own way of making steak, different from that of anyplace else in the world, and it starts from the moment the cow is born and ends when the beef enters your mouth. When the CEO is on top of things and is not lazy, the cow will grow into the perfect steak.

BUT HOW *DO* YOU VALUE A COMPANY?

The "choose yourself-er" needs to know how to value a company as a starting point to any negotiation. If you are smarter about how you value a company, then you have an edge in any negotiation. You're smarter *because* you have the ideas, which give you information and provide an advantage.

Forget about stocks for a second. Many people think that the way they value stocks is the way they should value companies. Stocks on the stock market are tiny slivers of a company. Warren Buffett often says that if you buy a stock you should think of yourself as an *owner* of a company. This might be true, but unless you're someone like Warren Buffett, you're not really an owner in the traditional sense. An owner has power. An owner can fire people, direct a change in strategy, improve the product, and so on. An owner chooses himself and can move the company more toward the top right quadrant of the idea matrix (see figure).

FIG. 1: THE IDEA MATRIX

● Franchisee		● Artists	● → • Idea Machines • Great Artists • Successful Entrepreneurs
● Guy who made Gmail for Google		● "Solopreneurs"	
● "Entre-ployees"			
		● "Disobedience"	• Lawyers • Stockbrokers • Mediocre Consultants or Coaches
● Employee/Idea Slave			● →

GOOD ⇧⇧⇧⇧⇧ BAD

WORKING ON OTHER PEOPLE'S IDEAS ⇨ ⇨ ⇨ ⇨ ⇨ GIVING OTHER PEOPLE GOOD IDEAS

A shareholder is just along for the ride—basically an idea slave. He owns stock and must depend on the good graces of the real owners to make money. A shareholder can move from the bottom left/idea slave quadrant to the bottom right quadrant (or higher) by owning shares of many companies and diversifying—but let's assume for a second we're talking about valuing a company for the sake of really owning it or making a deal where our profits are, in part, dependent on our own actions. There are many models by which you can value a company. I'm going to discuss three of them in detail.

THE *ZERO TO ONE* APPROACH

P eter Thiel has written an excellent book about what I will call *super en-trepreneurship* called *Zero to One*. I had the good fortune to discuss the contents of Peter's book in depth when I had him on my podcast. He highlights the four qualities of a good business—but it's important to note that he's not *valuing* a business. His goal is to *make* a great business—not just a great business but also a world-changing business. And there's almost no way to value a world-changing business. It can be priceless.

Thiel's four attributes for a good business are monopoly, scalability, network effect, and brand.

MONOPOLY

T his one is a funny one because technically the word *monopoly* stirs up nega-tive feelings of antitrust legislation, the government stepping in, anti-com-petition, AT&T in the '80s, Microsoft in the '90s, price manipulation, and even anti-capitalism. The genius of Peter's perspective, however, is that it's the exact op-posite. Capitalism, he says, is about profits. If everyone is competing, the service or product you are selling becomes a commodity and profits quickly go as tiny as they possibly can. He therefore concludes that competition is anti-capitalist.

Thiel isn't suggesting price manipulation or anything like that. He just sug-gests doing the following: find your niche, then find a small or a nonexistent market where you can enter and dominate 80 percent of the market, as if you were a monopoly. Two examples that immediately come to mind are companies he's either started or invested in: PayPal and Facebook. Peter had a vision of a cashless economy. He wanted people to be able to e-mail payments back and forth to each other over the Internet rather than exchange cash or (worse) private credit card information. Although the service was available to every retailer and consumer, he found a niche market where many online transactions were occurring and he decided to build his monopoly there: eBay customers. Why shouldn't every eBay customer use PayPal to settle their transactions? Only two things stood in his way: eBay could compete and Peter had one competitor, X.com, run by Elon Musk. So rather than try to directly destroy his competitors, Peter reinforced that PayPal was a monopoly. First off, he paid customers who signed up ten dollars. This basically killed off eBay's efforts almost immediately.

Second, he merged with X.com. Why merge with a company he could potentially defeat? When you have a fifty-fifty merger like that your percentage ownership gets diluted. I see too many entrepreneurs worry about dilution and fight to the bone for it.

You'll recall from an earlier chapter that when I was making a deal with TheStreet to distribute Stockpickr on their site, I told them I thought they should take 3 to 10 percent. CEO Tom Clarke laughed and responded, "We were thinking 50 percent." I didn't even think twice about it before saying, "OK." In fact, TheStreet.com taking 50 percent was a much better deal for me than their taking 3 percent. There are several reasons for this:

- First is the cliché that 1 percent of something is better than 100 percent of nothing. I saw other companies in which TheStreet.com had invested that ended up being worth nothing because they over-negotiated on percentages — which led to . . .
- TheStreet.com had an incentive to make the company work. Because they would own 50 percent, my revenues and earnings would show up on their earnings statements. In other words, they HAD to make it work. Every single page on their site (which got a billion visits a year) had a link to my site. All of their advertisers ended up advertising on my site.

• When I was negotiating to sell the company, they weren't just a passive investor waiting to be bought out. They were dreading that I was finding them an unwelcome new partner. So instead of letting me sell the other 50 percent, they had to go in and buy the other 50 percent less than five months after we launched our deal.

The other company they invested in around the same time ended up going out of business. TheStreet.com only owned 10 percent of them.

So Peter Thiel naturally figured, why fight Elon Musk's X.com and destroy each other in the process plus waste a ton of time and money when they could just merge and become a monopoly and go public and create real value, even if meant they all had lesser stakes? Once they merged they had twice as many ideas — which meant that their stakes would be worth *more* than twice as much, since we now know that ideas are more valuable than money. So they merged, went public, and guess what? eBay acquired them for $1.5 billion. Peter Thiel's final stake was worth $55 million. He didn't become a billionaire there but his savvy moves had created wealth for generations.

I asked him about Facebook, which he didn't really talk a lot about in his book, at least in relation to the monopoly question. I wanted to know — wasn't Facebook just an incremental improvement over MySpace, which itself was an incremental improvement over Friendster, Geocities, etc.

No, he said. Facebook was the first social network to force you to use your *true identity*. It had a monopoly on social networks that focused on real identity. And it started in its small niche, Harvard, and slowly expanded out, dominating one market at a time before expanding further.

Here's where we can veer off. Peter Thiel is a game changer. With each idea, he wants to not only create a monopoly. He has a vision and wants to see everyone in the world be a part of that vision in the long run.

Think of how this relates to the chain of pizza stores discussed in the prior section. Domino's is always a natural monopoly in whatever college town it goes into. If you are in a college dormitory and want to order pizza, then there's probably a 50 percent chance the first place you think to call is Domino's. As soon as you open up and distribute some flyers on campus, you'll get calls that night and make back all of your marketing costs. The key for a good monopoly is that it doesn't need to market much because it's the only game in town. If competition opens up, they are going to have be extra special to compete against a Domino's or they will quickly go out of business, like most restaurants (since restaurants are rarely monopolies).

When you value a business, you have to ask — where is it a monopoly? What divisions that are not monopolies can you sell off? What new areas can you move it into that will make it a monopoly? What companies can it buy? Etc.

∽

SCALABILITY

Can you "make money while you sleep"?

In other words, can you add customers at almost no additional cost or effort while you're off in dreamland? A platform like PayPal or Facebook has almost zero additional cost when it adds customers. A company like Domino's is not as scalable but it's still scalable, since I can hire more low-cost labor as customers ramp up and I can buy more locations. Again, there are more costs involved so you'll need to factor this into your decision about whether this is a good or a bad business. Are you comfortable with the costs of expansion?

By the way, even if you never scale, then you also fit into the *idea matrix*. If you have good ideas but don't want to scale, you'll find yourself dead center on the top of the idea matrix. You're not really going out of your way to come up with many ideas to help lots of people, but you have good ideas and ideas make money. There are many "lifestyle entrepreneurs" that like their one particular idea and don't want to replicate it and just want to make enough to get buy. For instance, someone who hand makes furniture can fit into this category. Or a gym where the trainer likes his training program, enjoys training people, and doesn't want to franchise it. Franchising an idea makes something scalable. Having one physical location makes it not scalable.

NETWORK EFFECT

The more people who use a service, the more valuable it is. It's not a business, but e-mail has the network effect going for it. The more people who signed up for e-mail, the more valuable it was that you also had to sign up for e-mail in order to communicate with everyone. Facebook and PayPal, as you may now have guessed, had the network effect. Domino's, believe it or not, had the network effect. Where would you rather order from—the same place all your friends' trust, or some random place that nobody has ever used before? And these three attributes are intimately connected to Peter Thiel's fourth attribute of a successful business.

BRAND

I mentioned before in this book that people would prefer to buy an item on Amazon rather than your own personal site (even if it's more expensive on Amazon) simply because Amazon is known as a trusted site. And so it is with the Domino's brand as a reliable deliverer of pizza.

Apple's brand has a significant reputation for focusing on design. They don't always have the best products — but often, when they catch up to competitors, they end up with a better-designed, good product, which gives them an edge. Again, Thiel focuses primarily on world-changing businesses. I've probably never interviewed a greater visionary and I probably never will. But every business in the world fits into these categories and you can begin your valuations here. Part of the process of valuing something is saying: "OK, it's not a monopoly but it will cost me $X to make it one." And that's part of your equation of determining a value to offer for a business. In the case of the Domino's Pizza chain that my friend was buying, the previous owners had been ruining their brand by not delivering on time and not having round pizzas. This was critical to the Domino's brand. With businesses like Domino's—in an industry where it's easy to compete—brand might be everything. In fact, brand is so important that the company was being run into the ground simply because they were not sticking to it. And once he bought the business, all he had to do was fix the brand to completely turn around the franchises.

I am going to add one more variable to Peter Thiel's four items, and it might be the most important.

∽

DEMOGRAPHICS

It doesn't matter if you have the above four items. If you had a business that relied on training horses for horse-and-buggy cab services, then you were going to go out of business in the early 1900s as everything moved over to cars.

Warren Buffett is an example of a *demographics* investor. Even if a company's management is awful, the brand is awful, the competition is tough, and on and on, but still, the demographics are growing, he'll buy it—so even an idiot can run the business successfully. For instance, when Coke was having troubles Buffett made his biggest investment ever in Coca-Cola. How come? Because he realized that sooner or later everyone in the world would want to drink his favorite sweet drink. When American Express was mired in scandal in the early '60s, Warren Buffett sat down next to the cash register at his favorite steak house and saw how many people were using the American Express card as opposed to paying with cash. He realized that we were moving toward a credit card economy and put one-third of his hedge fund in the business, resulting in probably his best return of the 1960s. This was probably the one investment that set him on the path to permanent wealth. Demographics can work in your favor even in a small town or a lifestyle business. If a small town doesn't have a laundromat, and if you open one up, you can be pretty confident you'll have customers. If your laundromat is unique in any way, then perhaps you can scale it. Everyone needs to do laundry. That said, if another laundromat opens up next door, you might be in trouble, which is why you have to do everything you can to create a natural monopoly in your area first.

THE THREE D'S MODEL

Very rarely do you want to buy a company that is at the top of its game, since this usually means you are paying the most expensive price and many things can go wrong.

So what allows a company to be bought for cheap? I touched on this briefly in a prior chapter, but this is a model that has been in use for centuries to buy businesses and it often works. Find a business that satisfies the "three D's":

- Death
- Divorce
- Debt

If the founder of a business dies and the children are off doing other things, often they will be willing to sell it cheap rather than watch it run into the ground. When founders get divorced, they often have to sell the business at any cost in order to divide up the assets and end their marriage. And finally, if a company is in debt and for whatever reason starts to go down because it starts lacking in the five qualities mentioned above, then you may be able to buy that company super cheap. Sometimes you just have to take over the debt and you've bought the company.

I was talking to Marcus Lemonis, the CEO of Camping World, who has bought hundreds of companies. He is also the star of the TV show *The Profit*, where he helps struggling companies turn around and he always gets skin in the game by writing them a check out of his own account.

I suggested to him that it seemed like all his purchases were related to the "three D's." And he gave me one more D: Delay.

Often companies get paralyzed when they have to make critical decisions, and the resulting delay can start driving their value down until they are in trouble. For instance, if two brothers are running a business and aren't getting along they will often delay on critical decisions.

I bring Marcus up for a specific reason. Before you can value a company, you have to also see what it takes to turn the company around. Turning it around doesn't necessarily mean turn it into a monopoly.

When Peter Thiel focuses on monopolies it's because he wants to start businesses where the sky is the limit. But when you buy a company, you probably want to make more money than you spent on it. You want to have better ideas than the prior owner so you can simply improve the company. It may not become a monopoly, but maybe you can improve it over its competition so it seems more like a monopoly. Or you may want to figure out the cost to improve the brand. Or you may want to see how to make it more scalable. Or it might even be simpler than that.

The Three P's Model

When Marcus values a company he uses a model he calls the Three P's. If you watch his show on CNBC, you will see him repeat the three P's in every episode.

- People
- Process
- Product

A company will probably be failing (and hence need a financial partner) if the people running it are no good, if the Process is inefficient or too expensive, and if the product is poor or doesn't stand out against the competition. "In 100 percent of cases," Marcus told me, "it starts with the people." This is usually because the people running the business are the ones who need to come up with the ideas on process and product.

So Marcus will often take an ownership stake, reorganize the people managing the company, and then use his own ideas to improve the process and the product. Since he's done this hundreds of times, he's an idea machine and is usually more qualified than the prior owners, which is why they take his financial deal.

So, after all that, how do you value a business?

Honestly, nobody has a clue. As they say, it's more art than science.

Why did Facebook pay $19 billion for WhatsApp, a company with no revenues whose CEO had actually been rejected by Facebook for a job just a few years earlier? I have a guess as to how they made the decision but still, that value might be right, or horribly wrong—making it either the best valuation decision or the worst in history. Here's what I do to value a business. I look at all of the above:

- The Peter Thiel Four—Monopoly, Scalability, Network Effect, Brand (and I'll add my Demographics)
- The Three D's. I look at what is causing the problems: Death, Divorce, Debt, Delay (because they all add up to a fifth D: Desperation, which drives prices lower)
- The Marcus Turnaround Method. I look at Product, Process, People—each one of those will have a cost but each one of will improve a company in the eyes of the Peter Thiel Four.

Then I ask myself, what does the company look like when it's turned around or made better?

What's the size of the market and how much will I dominate it? If it's scalable, how much is it scalable and what's the value of the additional markets it can scale to?

196

And I simply figure out how much money I can make out of this company in a certain period of time, minus what I have to put into it to keep it running or to turn it around.

Then I divide by half. Then I divide by half again. This makes it as safe as possible for me. So, if I think a company is worth $1,000 but I pay $250 for it, I've given myself a lot of room for safety.

By the way, I do the same for stocks. But, again, it's a little different because I can't control the ideas flowing into any company, so I might give myself even greater room for safety. A stock has to be really cheap by my standards in order for me to even look at it. For instance, Exxon might be a great company and even a cheap stock but I would never look at it. Not cheap enough.

If I'm trying to *sell* a company, I'll do the reverse. I'll demonstrate how much money the buying company can make given our status as a monopoly combined with *their* customer base. Always use the bigger customer base to value your company. Then divide in half and then divide in half again.

I've thrown in a lot of ways to look at a company here. How to value a start-up. How to value an old industry company. How to turn around a declining company. And how I value a company. Plus, I've shared the models I think are most important when assessing companies.

You might have different ideas or different models. For instance, you might love the hotel business, so no matter what the price, you're going to buy the hotel in your town. That's fine.

The methods I've outlined above are for the "Choose Yourself" person who wants to find a cheap asset, apply money and ideas to it, and then become wealthy as a result. Of course, we know, it's not always about the money. You will need to love being in business. But money is a great side effect of the ideas and effort you put into this.

Knowing the art and a little bit of the science of valuation is the key to making a lot more money than you put out. This is about how you take an asset that is far from the top right corner of the idea matrix and you move it closer to the top right corner. Once you do that, money appears, opportunities appear, abundance automatically happens. This applies no matter what—whether you are doing a tech start-up, a media company, a laundromat, a car wash company, whatever. And note that this is how I would start my valuation process of a company. If you want to "choose yourself" and you want to do it by owning businesses, this is the approach I would recommend. It beats sitting in a cubicle saving up money for a future that might not exist.

But valuation is only part one of how you buy a company. Next, I'll show you how to structure the deal. Just because you know something is now worth $X doesn't mean you'll pay $X for it. Your goal is to bake even more safety in and pay a lot less than $X.

Buy a Company for Free Without Any Experience, and Become a Billionaire
I have to admit: I've always been jealous of Richard Branson. I don't know if you remember that feeling when you were a kid and you were curious what sex was all about so you sneaked a look at some magazines in the pharmacy before they caught you and threw you out? Uhhh, I'm not saying that's happened to me. But I felt the same way when I read Branson's book *Losing My Virginity*.

Branson is a great example of the ultimate "Choose Yourself" deal: you get from here to there with *no money*. You buy something for free and with no experience. People often say they have a ton of ideas, but they just have trouble taking action. This is not true. Action ideas are a subset of ideas. In fact, you can have action ideas before you have a good idea.

Richard Branson was in his early twenties. He had a record magazine and a record label and a few other businesses. He wasn't a well-known name. He was, fittingly enough, in the Virgin Islands and he needed to get to Puerto Rico that night. The flight was canceled. But rather than focus on rebooking, he found a private plane that was available for a certain price. He didn't have the money on him. He put up a sign that said "Virgin Airways $39 to Puerto Rico" and he showed the sign to everyone who was on the canceled flight. He sold out the private plane and made it to Puerto Rico that night.

Then, he called Boeing and basically leased a plane from them the same way you would lease a car. He knew that if the business wasn't profitable, he could return the plane. He negotiated a route between Gatwick and Newark and he had a one-plane airline.

Branson started with nothing and did it. He offered services that no other airline did (the thirteen airlines that told him he was crazy to compete with them have *all* since gone out of business). Then he begged and borrowed to buy another plane, and another. And now he has Virgin Galactic ready to send people into space.

There's no single path that works for everyone, no one easy way to structure things. Branson could've bought an existing airline. He could've bought some planes and bought some routes. He could've taken out a heavy loan. But each step of the way he tried to do it cheap and with an element of fun—and that's how he always got the best deal and why he's still in business now.

You want to be trading ideas and value for money every step of the way. Very few deals go like this: "Here's $X for your product or company." I've reviewed *standard* negotiation in the chapter on negotiating, and I go over standard types of structures in "A Cheat Sheet for Starting and Building a Business." But always remember that life is not a straight line.

Back in 1999, I wanted to buy a software company because I thought I wanted to be in the wireless Internet space. I made thirty calls to companies. Twenty-nine of them said no. One company said "Yes, but Ericsson, the phone giant, is about to buy us for $17 million." I said, "I'll pay you $30 million." I didn't *have* $30 million. I didn't have any million. But I wasn't lying to them. We made a deal. I had a certain amount of time to get the $30 million or the deal was off.

First I met with Ericsson, and some of their executives actually gave me part of the $30 million. Now I had a real company. What were my assets? Barely anything. I had an agreement to buy a company for $30 million and I had a partner in Ericsson. Using those meager assets I raised money from Henry Kravis, Investcorp, CMGI, Allen & Co., and about a dozen other high-profile investors. Many deals are like that: what comes first, the chicken or the egg?

Nineteen out of twenty deals don't work out. Nineteen out of twenty of anything doesn't work out. But so do twenty things. Or as Scott Adams, creator of *Dilbert*, told me, so do two hundred things. Something will eventually work out, because luck favors the prepared, the persistent, and (I need a third P), the *promiscuous*. There! I think I pulled it off—be promiscuous with ideas. Go for every idea that excites you, and for every deal you can find. There is always time for excitement and fun.

When Scott Adams was stuck in his cubicle he tried every idea to get out of there and almost every idea failed. Finally, he returned to a passion of his from when he was ten years old: cartooning. You can see his first fifty *Dilbert* cartoons on his blog. I don't want to make a judgment but I think you can even see what he thinks of those first fifty. But this was one of his two hundred attempts to break out of prison and choose himself. As he described to me, he got rejected almost everywhere. Finally, the decision maker at United Media called him. She said she didn't like the cartoons but her husband, who worked at IBM, had seen them on the floor of her car, picked them up, and started laughing. So now she wanted to do a deal. Scott wanted to sound like he was doing serious due diligence so he asked her, "Well, can you tell me other comic strips you represent."

He said to me, "There was this long pause at the other end. And finally she said, 'Well, we represent *Peanuts, Calvin & Hobbes…*'"

"'OK,' I told her, and that was the end of my due diligence." And now he's in 2,000 papers across the world, six days a week.

A friend of mine named Marni Kyrnis was telling me how she was miserable in her PR job. I believe I've already used PR jobs as the worst-level jobs on the bottom left quadrant of the Idea Matrix. Often, people who have no right to be in the media's eye at all hire a PR firm because they want to be famous and they have absolutely zero ideas or reasons for being known. It's then the PR professional's job to come up with ideas (and all of them will be bad) to get their client into the news.

Marni went out to a mixer one night and saw that the men were standing on one side and the women were standing on the other side. "It was like a junior high school prom," she told me. So she went over to the men and one by one walked them over to who she thought the appropriate woman would be and introduced them. "By the end of the evening everyone was dancing, exchanging numbers, even making out in the corner," she said. "My mind was buzzing when I got home. I had found what I wanted to do. I wanted to help guys meet women because they were totally incompetent at it. My roommate told me I was crazy. But I put an ad on Craigslist that said, 'I will be your wing girl at the bar.'" She listed a charge of some outrageous amount in the ad and then went to sleep. When she woke up she had seventy-five replies and a new career.

Then she wanted to scale it, so she started selling videos to guys telling them how they could meet women. And she built up her brand by writing and podcasting her experiences. Now she has a perfect "Choose Yourself" career.

It doesn't matter if you're Peter Thiel investing in Facebook. Or Richard Branson starting an airline. Or me starting seventeen businesses in a row that failed before finding a few that succeeded. Or Marni, making a career out of being a "wing girl." When you have ideas, you'll quickly get freedom. When you get freedom, you'll have the energy to build more ideas, to generate more abundance, to live the life you want to live.

PART 3

KEEP AND GROW THE MONEY YOU MAKE

THE MYTHS WE'VE ALL BEEN TOLD

Most of us (e.g., me) fail because we believed a story and it didn't work out for us.

Here's what happened, and it's a good thing: in order for you and I to cooperate, even if we are total strangers, we need to believe in a story together. Our brains tell us we can both trust each other, for instance, if we believe in the Bible, even if we are strangers and speak different languages. In the history of the world, for three billion years, this has only happened ONCE: with the human species and only over the past 40,000 or so years. That's how we went from the middle of the food chain to the top. That's how we went from nomadic tribes without the ability to tell stories, to global civilizations. But because storytelling is only the latest programming inside of our DNA there are many "bugs" or fatal flaws.

We're not so good at it yet, so when stories like "nationalism" or "ideologies" or "religions" break down we end up with wars and death and despair. That is how our DNA weeds out the bad storytellers from the good storytellers. The DNA doesn't care who lives and who dies.

But you and I care. It was that familiar story about the old way and the old approach, the "American Dream" so many embraced for so many years. We know by now that this isn't the way things are anymore. And the good news is this: if you can become aware of the myths that people hold and the way they manipulate societies and cultures, you can write your own rules and create abundance for yourself. This book has (hopefully) already given you a lot of ideas on how to do this. But the myths will persist, for a while anyway. Every single myth listed below costs people millions or makes them millions.

If you think of any I've missed, please tell me. Each one of these myths can lead to entire businesses, can lead to happiness if you are aware of them, can lead to less stress if you understand how the myth manipulates its way through our society.

1. Owning a home will give you "roots," and is far better than "flushing money down the toilet with rent." Most people don't realize that owning a home has all the attributes of the worst investment possible: it's highly illiquid, there's a high leverage, it includes most of your net worth, and provides you with an average return of only 0.2 percent over the past year. And this doesn't count all your maintenance costs. I'd rather rent, and either invest the extra money in myself and my own ideas.

2. Going to college is a pretty safe guarantee of getting a job, and leads to more money and happiness than if you don't go to college. Right now more than 50 percent of unemployed people have some college experience. College is no guarantee of anything. Debt keeps rising and it's a waste of four years of a child's life. There are so many ways to learn better and for free now on the Internet while you can spend the time exploring the world, exploring your interests, making friends, or doing whatever you want to do while you have the energy to do it.

3. Getting married means you won't be alone. (you might still feel alone if married. I'm not saying marriage is bad. Just that it is a myth that it solves loneliness.)

4. Having kids is the purpose of life, and having a purpose in life is important to having a fulfilling life. I like how Scott Adams from Dilbert fame put it: live according to Systems and not Goals. Nobody has a single purpose in life. We are often put into our life circumstances and have to figure out how to do the best. In this book and in *Choose Yourself!* I try to give a system to develop great ideas and build abundance.

5. My family is my "family."

6. You have to be dishonest to be successful.

7. Giving to a "a charity" is the same as being charitable.

8. You need to vote if you want to change the world.

9. Procrastination is bad

10. Needing little sleep is good and allows for greater productivity

11. There is no connection between the mind and the body.

12. One religion is correct.

13. One diet will lead to health.

14. You can change the world without first changing yourself.

15. If you work hard, you can succeed.

16. Success has something to do with money.

17. I'll never die (didn't learn that was wrong until my thirties, actually)

18. I can do X later. Where X is the thing you love doing the most.

19. I can't X. One percent of the time this is true. But 99 percent of the time it's false. And 99 percent of the time people believe it.

20. Stop signs save lives. Not only is this is a myth but so are all the times when people say, "Stop."

21. You need to know what you are going to do with your life by age X, where " is some arbitrary age. Usually people think it's in their twenties.

22. Humans are smarter now than they were 40,000 years ago.

23. Sometimes wars can be justified.

24. Happiness is better than tranquility.

25. If you act like yourself people might not like you.

26. A job brings stability or wealth.

27. Money solves all of your money problems.

28. There is one "right" way of doing things In any situation. Of course sorting through the haze of BS to find the needle of truth requires a new way of looking at things, and it is uncomfortable because it gets you out of what we are used to doing.

How to Avoid The Great Financial Scam of the Twenty-First Century

When it comes to investing, we tend to follow what the people before us have done. Many people have their money in the US stock market, and the US stock market consistently hits all-time highs. Yes, we went through a period in 2008–2009 where it was pretty scary to hold stocks. But less than five years later we were hitting all-time highs every week. Will we continue to hit all-time highs? I don't know. We've been doing it for two hundred years, so we might keep doing it. There are a lot of times when people claim that "this time it's different," and one of these days they will be right.

But in case you are going to put some money in stocks, we'll talk about that in a second. First, let's look at some common criminal, or at least dubious, behavior that the banks, the brokers, the government, the lawyers, the corporations, the mutual funds, the hedge funds, the funds of funds, the ETFs, the Federal Reserve, would rather you didn't know about. First, I'll tell you a story.

One of the largest investors of a public company called me up the other day. He said to me, "James, the Nasdaq wants to know how someone could short 10 percent of our stock in the final minute of trading. How is that even possible?" This man, who is a good friend of mine, owns about $800 million worth of his company. I said to him, David, do you allow your broker to lend out your shares to short sellers?"

He paused. "I'm not sure what that means," he said.

I said, "Well, in order for someone to short your stock, at some point they have to have the stock they are shorting in their hands. Shorting is the same as selling. You can't sell something you don't have your hands on."

He said, "James, my broker is the most prestigious bank in the world"—he named a bank here that is at least in the top three or four of the most prestigious banks in the world—"and I'm a huge customer for them. Why would they lend out my shares to anyone that would hurt me?"

I said, "Because they charge interest on that and make money, and because you've never asked them to split that money with you they get to pocket that money. You own a lot of stock so it's great for them to get people to short a ton of your stock because they can lend out all of your stock and charge 10 to fifteen percent interest on it."

"No way. They don't do that."

"Just call them tomorrow and ask. And then tell them you are not allowing them to do that, no matter what they say."

The next day David called me again. "James, I asked them and they were dead silent. Then my broker said, 'Dave, I have to call you back.' And now it's the end of the day and nobody's called me back."

The very next day after that, his stock was up fifteen percent.

There are lots of things happening in the above story that explain how Wall Street works. And by the way, I'm not bashing Wall Street or saying everything about it is bad. Wall Street helps companies raise money, and companies that raise money can hire people and invent new products and services and do all sorts of fun things.

But I don't want to play in their sandbox, whether I have one hundred dollars or $800 million.

First off, why was someone shorting my friend's stock in the last minute of trading?

Easy: the short seller wanted to scare people at the open the next day. People would be shocked into selling, and the short seller could buy back his shares at a lower price, pocketing a nice profit.

Well why would the bank lend the shares, thereby hurting their customer?

Because they charge anywhere from 5 percent up to 50 percent (!) interest in some cases. And if the customer is not aware of it, even he's one with $800 million, then they don't split it with their customer.

Every bank does this all day long to every customer.

Well, you might say, I have my money in a mutual fund. So I bet the bank doesn't lend out the shares the mutual fund owns.

Wrong. But in this case the mutual fund is sophisticated. The mutual fund says, "Excuse me, bank, can I please split that with you and we won't tell anyone?" So mutual funds benefit by taking some of the interest when they lend the shares to the short seller. This is actually a pretty safe way to make money on Wall Street: to be in the business of lending shares.

Should this type of lending be made illegal?

No, of course not. Short selling has often been the way that smart investors have exposed scams like Enron and Worldcom by giving them financial incentives to do so.

Is it abused? Yes, it is—like every other aspect of Wall Street.

But if this is what one of the largest banks in the world is going to do with someone who has $800 million in the bank, then you really have to ask yourself:

What are they currently doing to *you?*

Your next question is likely, well, what about Roth IRAs, 401(k)s, employer-matching programs, etc., etc.?

I have no clue. But I'll tell you what I think.

First off, here's what happens with all of these programs:

1. You get an income for about five seconds.

2. Your company puts your hard-earned income into a plan that you can't touch until you're sixty-five years old.

But, you're thinking, it's *mine*, right?

Nope—not until you are sixty-five. The only things that are yours are *things you can hold in your hand.* They will *tell* you it's yours but the fine print describes penalties if you want to hold that money in your hands—in some cases, *huge penalties.*

So if it's not mine, then where does my hard-earned money go?

Well, a 401(k) plan will invest in a mutual fund.

Here's what happens to money in a mutual fund.

Some of the money goes into buying stocks. When someone buys a stock, another person sells a stock. So your money went straight from your employer, to a 401(k) plan to a mutual fund to someone selling a stock who needs to buy his boat. At that point, you can good-bye to that money.

Some of the money sits in cash in the bank. The bank either charges fees on that money or lends it out. After all, that's how a bank makes money? So some of your hard-earned money might be going into the hands of either a bank manager's salary or someone borrowing the money from a bank to buy a house or a car. This is what's happening to your money.

And some of the money goes into the hands of the people who manage the mutual fund, right? Then, some of the money goes into expenses that are set aside to market the mutual fund. They are allowed a certain amount to buy ads in magazines, etc.

I'm not exaggerating anything here. This is how Wall Street works:

1. You earned money by working hard.
2. You had the money in your hands for half a second.
3. Now your money is all over Wall Street being spent at wild champagne orgies while you wait until you are an old man (or nearing old age) before you can touch your money again).

There is a con for every pro. Yes, your money might go up in huge amounts and allow you to retire as a very rich person. Or it might not. Some plans do well, some don't. It's a lot of work to figure out what works and what doesn't, let alone what's going to be working between now and when you are sixty-five.

Meanwhile, I just told you what's happening to your hard-earned money *right now.*

One more thing you might be wondering, and it's a great question: what if your employer matches the money you put in your IRA? It's as if you're doubling your money—right?

First off, they don't do that with all of your money. Second, most people don't stay at jobs long enough anymore for them to really benefit from it. Third, for me personally, I still rest easier not handing over my money until I'm sixty-five. I'm forty-six now. I can die tomorrow. I like to see the money I work for.

What if I want to take out all my money in the form of two-dollar bills, fill up my swimming pool with the money, and dive right into it? Heck, I want to have that option. And you might want to have it also.

Takeaway: every fancy retirement plan is a way to transfer money straight from your employer to Wall Street professionals, bypassing you along the way. This is a different question, by the way, than "Should I put my money in the stock market?"

But as we move into a "Choose Yourself" economy, you need to take control over what happens to your personal assets. Nobody else is looking out for you. You have to look out for you.

The US government has laws that allow "sophisticated" or what they call "accredited" investors to invest differently than "unsophisticated." Some vehicles that sophisticated investors invest in include hedge funds, funds of hedge funds, derivatives, venture capital funds, private equity funds. Bernie Madoff's fund, for instance, was made up entirely of sophisticated investors.

Right now, get down on your hands and knees and pray to God or Allah or Buddha or whoever if you are an unsophisticated investor.

A fraud doesn't become a *huge* fraud unless it has the blessings of many sophisticated investors.

If you give me the year, I can give you a scam that took place. In the '90s it was Reg S trading, and everyone involved went to jail. In the early 2000s it was mutual fund timing. In the late 2000s it was PIPEs. In the later 2000s it was insider trading.

Of course there were plenty of Ponzi schemes, of which Madoff is the worst. And, of course, a Ponzi scheme has many victims.

For instance, me.

I was not invested in Madoff. But I was running what's called a fund of hedge funds at the time. This means an investor would invest money with me, I'd charge a fee, I'd then invest the money in hedge funds I did due diligence on, and they would all charge me fees.

Forget that the initial investor is now paying 1 percent to me and then 2 percent to all the funds I invest in, plus a percentage of the profits to all the hedge funds I invest in (since hedge funds are allowed to charge on a percentage of profits, unlike mutual funds for unsophisticated investors).

Those fees on top of fees are evil enough.

But when I was trying to raise money, very smart people would say to me, "Why should I invest in you when I could invest in a great fund like Madoff?"

And I never had any answer to that.

In fact, I visited Bernie Madoff one time. He had a lot of employees up there. You know what he said to me? "One day, computers will be doing what all of these employees are doing."

Oh, he said another thing to me. He said, "I can't put money with you because I don't know where you are putting your money. The last thing we need to see is 'Bernard Madoff Securities' on the front page of the *Wall Street Journal*." And he was right. That is the last thing he needed to see.

Ultimately, I had to shut my fund down. Who could compete? So many legitimate funds that might have been better places for investor money (better to pay all the fees than lose all your money in a Ponzi scheme) couldn't survive because the illegitimate funds crowded them out of the space.

Some vehicles that "sophisticated investors" invest in: hedge funds, funds of hedge funds, derivatives, venture capital funds, private equity funds.

Other than the Ponzi schemes and super-fees charged by all these entities, here is the dark secret that none of these funds will tell you: when the market goes up, all of these funds do well. When the market goes down, pretty much all of these funds go down. There are exceptions, but that's the case with any broad statement. In most cases, all of these sophisticated vehicles are highly correlated with the US stock market, which is highly correlated with global markets.

Everything I've said so far in this chapter might suggest that I like John Bogle's approach.

John Bogle is a hero for many in the investment community. He is the founder of the Vanguard funds, which charge super-low fees to be fairer to the investor. This is not such a bad approach.

However, you still often have to pay fees to the bank to buy into his funds. There's still an annual fee (albeit very low) and there's till this nonsense about lending out their shares so people can short the stocks they own (to be fair, I don't know if Vanguard does this but many funds like Vanguard do).

Again, I'm not saying "do" or "don't" (yet). But I will tell you exactly what I do with almost all of the shares I own. Not every share, but the bulk.

I'm sitting right now at a little white desk, typing into a computer. The desk has two drawers. In one drawer I keep stacks of two-dollar bills just in case I need to make a coffee run to the local café.

In the other drawer is the physical shares of stocks I own. They are beautiful. They are all nicely designed, and you know what I like? They have my name on them.

So I can do something almost nobody else in the United States can do. I can hold my money in my hands.

Stop Paying Your Debts

I'm going to give you one tip in this chapter to avoid going broke. There are a lot of tips actually that will help you. OK, I've just decided while writing this that I'm going to give two tips.

Tip #1: Never invest big chunks of your money.

A big chunk is more than 2 percent of your money. So if you have $10,000, don't buy a TV that costs more than two hundred dollars. Don't buy an iPad. Don't buy a car. Definitely don't buy a car. Just be happy with the money in the bank. But if you have even more money here's what it means:

- Don't go to college.
- Don't own a home.
- Don't invest more than 2 percent in any private company.
- Don't invest more than 2 percent in any stock or any bunch of stocks in the same sector (don't put more than 10 percent overall in stocks).
- Don't invest in your own company. I know one guy who had a big idea that he loved. He put a million a month into his own company. Had 40 employees. Slept with the secretary. Divorced his wife and married the secretary. Had two kids with the secretary. Divorced her. Married another secretary. Went broke. Disappeared.

These are common mistakes, by the way. I went broke several times doing most of the above at different parts of my "career." It would've been so easy to hold on to money. For instance, I could've played poker every night and held on to my money. Instead, an accountant told me, "What are you doing playing poker? You should be starting a business again!" So I did. I put money into my business. Into other people's businesses. Into stocks. And then a year later at three in the morning I was crying in the streets, "Why did I do that?" I was feeling so bad I lost 30 pounds. I weighed the same amount as I weighed in 8th grade. I lost everything. I would look at my 3 year old and think, "I just ruined your life." OK, enough of Tip #1. I hate that tip because if I had followed it, my whole life would've been different.

Tip #2. The whole point. Stop paying your debt. Let me clarify. If you borrowed from a friend, pay your friend back. Be a good person.

But all other debt is a contract, and there are several situations where you can stop paying debt. "Ethics" is a government-made term to try and induce you to pay back your debt when you don't have to. But you can ignore that.

HOUSE DEBT

If your house is underwater then stop paying back your debt. This isn't about ethics; it's common financial sense. You have a contract with the bank. Your "mortgage" is really "rent" until the bank no longer owns your house. If you stop paying it, then the bank will take your house. The good news is, you can stop paying and it will be a good eighteen months or more before the bank actually forces you out. There's various ways you can extend that eighteen months to be even longer, particularly if your house is underwater (your bank doesn't really want your house so even they will help you delay).

"But," you might say, "My credit will go bad." OK. It will. Who cares? Don't buy another house so fast.

"But," you might say, "It's really annoying that the bank will be calling me all the time." OK. I agree with that.

"But," you might say, "isn't it amoral?"

No. You agreed in a contract the exact thing that will happen if you don't pay back. The bank can take the *home you live in*. That's quite a bit you've agreed to give up. The bank has scammed you. And now your house is underwater and you're expected to keep paying them. So instead, you will give them something of great value. *Your shelter.* Have at it, bank. *You* try to fucking sell it.

———❧———

STUDENT LOAN DEBT

B*AM!* Student loan debt is now over $1.4 trillion. It should be zero. Y'all should stop paying down your student loan debt now. How come?

For one thing, it's better for the country. Much better for young people to be investing in their lives than giving that money back to the government.

It's better for *you.* You need a start. You don't need to be in more debt than everyone else when you're only twenty-two. It's crazy how much money you owe! The colleges scammed you. They knew that the government would be backing any loans to you so they upped tuitions ten times faster than inflation since 1977. You, sir or ma'am, are the victim of a con. And your own country will try to force you into bankruptcy if you don't pay. It's much better to stop paying this debt and use the money you save to make yourself a life, rather than be an indentured servant to the government for the rest of your life.

Let's send a message: the education wasn't worth it. Look at how many people are unhappy right now. And unemployed. Or making 50 percent less than what they made a few years ago, while everything else has inflated (the so-called "U5" measurement of unemployment).

Well, that's a lot of debt. I've just helped you forgive $16 trillion worth of debt. I hope you put that money to good use. Maybe by starting businesses, making inventions, feeling better, hiring people, and so on.

What about IRS debt? You have to pay that. The IRS will put you in jail if you don't. I don't agree with what they do with the money. They use my money to kill innocent babies in Afghanistan. But I can't do anything about it now. Maybe when my kids are older and I move away from here. Or maybe I'll sign up to go to Afghanistan. This way I can get some of my money back.

What else do you owe? Credit card debt? Screw it. Here's what happens to your credit card debt. The credit card company writes you down to three cents on the dollar within just three to six months of you not paying. They've already long forgotten you. They then sell your debt to a hedge fund. The hedge fund then outsources the collection to local lawyers or collection agencies in your area. They collect six to eight cents on the dollar. I know this because I've invested in several of these hedge funds. The hedge funds make 100 percent on that debt they buy. You never had to actually pay that back. What were they going to do? Seize your assets? Put your assets under another name? Why let a bunch of rich guys who invested in hedge funds get paid on your hard-earned dollars?

But? You might ask, won't I get bad credit?

Yeah, you will. Don't get a credit card ever again. What do you need that big TV for anyway? Only buy what you can afford. Don't be an idiot anymore. But, you might ask, if everyone followed this advice, won't the banking system go down the drain. And the answer is: yes, it will. But nobody will follow this advice. So don't worry about everyone else. Just worry about making sure you don't go broke so you can feed your family, yourself, start businesses, and take a step back and really enjoy your life before you die.

Life doesn't have to be just a bus station. Make decisions that are scary right now so you can have moments that are not only fun, but also funny, later on.

The Ultimate Guide To Investing

In the history of capitalism, this is the hardest time ever to invest. People are going broke, losing their jobs, and fear more than greed rules the news and tries to rule thoughts. In short: people are scared. And I do think the uncertainty is going to rise quickly so I wanted to put this note together. In 2001 and 2002 I lost all my money through bad investing. The same thing happened to me on a couple of occasions after that. So why should anyone listen to me about investing? You shouldn't. You shouldn't listen to anyone at all about investing. This is your hard-earned money. Don't blow it by listening to an idiot like me. Here's my experience (and perhaps I've learned the hard way about what NOT to do and a little bit about what TO do.):

I've run a hedge fund that was successful. I ran a fund of hedge funds, which means I've probably analyzed the track records and strategies of about 1000 different hedge funds. I've been a venture capitalist and a successful angel investor (I was a HORRIBLE venture capitalist though - but I put that under the category of "does not work well with others").I can't raise money anymore. Nor do I want to play that game. I don't BS about my losses and everyone else does. So I'm not in that business anymore. It's too much work to run a fund anyway. In the past 15 years I've tried every investing strategy out there. I honestly can't think of a strategy I haven't experimented with. I've also written software to trade the markets automatically and I did very well with that. And I've written several books on my experiences investing, with topics ranging from automatic investing to Warren Buffett, to hedge funds, to long-term investing (my worse-selling book, *The Forever Portfolio*, which has sold 399 copies since it came out in December 2008, including one copy for the entire last quarter).

Incidentally, why publish a book called "The Forever Portfolio" during the worst financial crisis in history. I begged my publisher (Penguin) to postpone but they couldn't. "It's in the schedule" was their magic incantation. Publishers largely suck. The good news is: they will never make back the advance. That said, all of the picks in that book have done excellently since then but the one thing I am proud of is that I made a crossword puzzle for the book. I don't know of any other investing book with a crossword puzzle in it. So, Ok! Let's get started.

Don't follow any of my advice. This is advice that I do and follow and it works for me.

A) Should I Daytrade?

Only if you are also willing to take all of your money, rip it into tiny pieces, make cupcakes with one piece of money inside each cupcake and then eat all of the cupcakes. Then you will get sick, and eat all of your money, but it will taste thrilling along the way. Which is what day-trading is.

Also, see the chapter on what happened to me when I day traded.

C) Well, Who Makes Money In The Market Then?

Three types of people:

1. People who hold stocks FOREVER. Think: Warren Buffett (has never sold a share of Berkshire Hathaway since 1967) or Bill Gates (he sells shares but for 20 years basically held onto his MSFT stock).
2. People who hold stocks for a millionth of a second (see Michael Lewis's book "Flash Boys" which I highly recommend.) This is borderline illegal and I don't recommend it.
3. People who cheat.

I've seen it for 20 years. I've seen every scam. I can write a history of scams in the past 20 years.

Without describing them, here's the history: Reg S, Calendar trading, Mutual fund timing, Death spirals, Front running, Pump and Dump, manipulating illiquid stocks, Ponzi schemes, and inside information. Inside information has always existed and always will exist.

One time I wanted to raise money for one of my funds. I went to visit my neighbor's boss. The boss had been returning a solid 12% per year for 20 years. Everyone wanted to know how he did it. "Get some info while you are there," a friend of mine in the business said when he heard I was visiting my neighbor's boss. The boss said to me, "I'm sorry, James. We like you and if you want to work here, then that would be great. But we have no idea what you would be doing with the money. And here at Bernard Madoff Securities, reputation is everything".So I didn't raise money from Bernie Madoff although he wanted me to work there. Later, the same friend who wanted me to get "info" and "figure out how he does it" said to me: "we knew all along he was a crook." Which is another thing common in Wall Street. Everybody knows everything in retrospect and nobody ever admits they were wrong. Show me a Wall Street pundit who says "I was wrong" and I'll show you...I don't know...something graphic and horrible and impossible [fill in blank].

D) So how can one make money in the market?

I told you about: #1. Pick some stocks and hold them forever.

E) What stocks should I hold?

Warren Buffett has some advice on this (and I know because I wrote THE book about him. A friend of mine who knows him told me my book was the only book that Buffett thought was accurate about him). He says, "if you think a company will be around 20 years from now then it is probably a good buy right now." I would add to that, based on what Warren does. It seems to me he has five criteria:

1. A company will be around 20 years from now.

2. At some point, company's management has demonstrated in some way that they are honest, good people. If you can get to know management even better.

3. The company's stock has crashed for some reason (think American Express in early 60s, which he loaded up on. Or Washington Post in the early 70s. Or Coca-Cola in the early 80s).

4. The company's name is a strong brand: American Express, Coke, Disney, etc.

5. Demographics play a strong role.

With Coke, Buffett knew that everyone in the world would be drinking sugared water before long. Who can resist? He also started buying furniture companies right before the housing boom. He knew that as the population in the US grows, people will need chairs to sit on. Note that Buffett is not what some people call a "Value investor". But I won't get into that discussion here.

F) WHAT ELSE?

One time I accidentally got an email that was intended for a famous well-known investor. It was from his broker and contained his portfolio. I can't say how this accident happened but it did. Of course, I opened the email. This is a man who writes about lots of stocks. His entire portfolio was in municipal bonds. I don't know whether or not municipal bonds are good investments. But I would look into stocks that are called "closed-end funds" that invest only in municipal bonds. They usually pay good dividends, usually trade for less than their cash or assets in the bank, and are fairly stable (it's very hard for a municipality to not pay back its debts for various reasons, some of them constitutional). But do a lot of research into the towns.

I'll tell you one story. I had an idea for a fund in 2008 when oil was crashing at the end of the year. Stocks / funds that invested in municipal bonds in Texas were getting destroyed. Somehow, because oil was going down, everyone naturally assumed that Texas was going to simply disappear. I researched every municipal bond out there and found a good set of Texan cities that were being sold off with everyone else even though they had nothing to do with oil. I pitched it to a huge investor who had told me he wanted to back me on any idea I could come up with. He loved the idea. He loved it so much he told me, "You're too late. We already have about $500 million in this strategy and we bought the very stocks you are recommending." They went up over 100% in the next six months while the world was still in financial collapse. So he made a lot of money. As for me, I didn't put a dime into my own strategy and made nothing.

G) Should I Put All of My Money in Stocks?

No, because you'll never know anything about a company and you won't get the kind of deals that Warren Buffett gets.

So use this guideline:

- No more than 3% of your portfolio in any one stock. But if the stock grows past 3% you can keep it. To quote Warren Buffett again: "If you have Lebron James on your team, you don't trade him away."
- No more than 30% of your portfolio in stocks (unless some of the stocks grow, in which case you just keep letting them grow).

G, Part 2) What if We are In a Bubble?

Bubbles don't mean anything. We had an Internet bubble in the 90s. Then a housing bubble. Bubbles, bubbles, bubbles. And if you just held through all of that, your stock portfolio would have been at an all time high last Friday. So ignore cycles and bubbles and ups and downs. And NEVER EVER read the news. The news has no idea about the financial world and what makes it tick. Any investing off the news is like taking out your eyes because you trust a blind person to drive you to work.

H) My Friend Has a Business Idea. Should I Invest in It?

Probably not. But if you want a checklist, make sure these four boxes can be checked:

- The CEO has started and sold a business before.
- The business is a sector with a strong demographic headwind behind it. (or is that a tailwind?)
- The company has revenues and/or profits.
- You are getting a really good deal. (This is subjective but you can look at similar companies and what they were valued at.)

Every time I have invested with this approach it's worked miracles. And every time I have not invested in this approach it's been a DISASTER. Like, a CLUSTERF*(*K

Claudia doesn't let me invest in a private company unless all four items on my checklist apply. Which is important because I tend to believe in everything people tell me. So I'm happy to invest in a time portal black hole machine.

I) What Do You Think of Bitcoin?

I think bitcoin has about a 1 in 100 chance of being a survivor. So I have 1% of my portfolio in bitcoin.

J) What About Metals as a Hedge Against Inflation?

No, they have zero correlation with inflation. The best hedge against inflation is the US stock market since about 60% of revenues of the S&P 500 come from foreign countries.

K) What About Metals Like Gold? Don't They Have Intrinsic Value?

The only currency in the history of mankind that had actual intrinsic value was when people traded barley in the markets of the ancient city of Ur. Since then, we've developed currencies that we had to have faith in their value. Every currency has faith and hope backing it. When people began to lose faith in US currency (in the Civil War), the words "In God We Trust" were put on the dollar bill to trick people into having faith in it. But if you're going to pick a metal, wait until the gold/silver ratio gets higher than it's historical average and buy silver. How come? Because silver is both a precious metal (like gold) and an industrial metal (also like gold, but much much cheaper). So there actually is some intrinsic value in silver.

I bought some silver bars back in 2005. But then lost them when I moved. That's why nobody should listen to me about investing.

L) What About Mutual Funds?

No. Mutual funds, and the bank representatives that push them, consistently lie about the fees they are charging. I know this from experience. One time I accompanied a friend of mine who had made some money (she was a model and had a good run for awhile) and was looking to invest it. She asked me to go with her to see her bank representative who had some "ideas". Because she was beautiful, I went with her to the bank. I didn't talk at all during the meeting but jotted down every time the bank guy lied. He lied five times. Afterwards I ex-plained each of the lies to her. What happened? She put all her money with the guy. "He's practically family". I can't argue with a good salesman. But he lied about the mutual funds' performance that he was pitching, the fees they were charging, the commissions he was charging, and a few more I can't remember now. I wrote an article about it in the Financial Times back then.

Fact: Mutual funds don't outperform the general market so better to invest in the general market without paying the extra layer of fees.

Use the criteria I describe above, pick 20 companies and invest.

M) What Are Some Good Demographic Trends?

1. The Internet. Yes, it's still growing.
2. Baby boomers retiring. They need special facilities to live in. They need bet-

ter cancer diagnostics and treatments.

3. Energy. The more people we have, the more energy we will consume. Go for energy sources that are profitable and don't need government subsidies. Whenever you depend on the government, you could get in trouble.

4. Temp staffing. Every company is firing people and replacing them with temp staffers.

5. Batteries. If you can figure out how to invest in Lithium, then go for it.

N) Is a House a Good Investment?

Everyone will disagree with me on this but the answer is an emphatic "NO!" It has all the qualities of a horrible investment:

a) Constant extra layers of fees and taxes that never go away (maintenance, property taxes, etc. that all rise with inflation).

b) Usually housing is too-large a percentage of someone's portfolio. Even just the down-payment ends up being the largest expense of someone's life.

c) Usually massive debt is involved.

If you can avoid, "a", "b", and "c" and don't mind the opportunity cost in the time required to maintain your house then go for it. Else, rent, and use the money you saved for other investments that will be less stressful and pay off more.

Fact: Housing has returned 0.2% per year in the past 100 years.

O) If No Housing and Only 30% of My Portfolio in Stocks, Then What Should I do with the Rest of My Money?

Why are you in such a rush to put all of your money to work? Relax! Don't do it! There's a saying "cash is king" for a reason. I will even say, "Cash is queen" because on the chessboard the king is just a figurehead and the queen is the most valuable piece. Cash is a beautiful thing to have. You can pay for all of your basic needs with it. You can sleep at night knowing there is cash in the bank. I love a stress-free life. When I look back at the past 15 years, the times when I've been most stressed are when I've been heavily invested and the times when I've been least stressed is when I had cash in the bank. With cash in the bank you can also invest in yourself.

P) What Does That Mean, "Invest in Myself?"

1. It costs almost nothing to start a business. Find something people want and start posting information about it on a blog and then upsell your services on the blog.

   Or write 1000 small books about different topics and publish them on Amazon. You can do this on the side while you learn and have a full time job and then when you are ready, you can jump to your other passive streams of income. Note: It takes a lot of work to find "passive" income but when it happens, it's worth it.

   These are some ideas. There are many others.

2. Invest in experiences rather than possessions. Figure out interesting and unique experiences you can have or places you can go to (but they don't always have to be places). Experiences pay much higher dividends than an extra TV or a nicer car.

3. Books. Reading is the best return on investment. You have to live your entire life in order to know one life. But with reading you can know 1000s of people's lives for almost no cost. What a great return!

Q) Should I Save Money With Each Paycheck?

No. Just try to make more money. That is easier than saving money. I find that whenever I try to save money I end up spending more. I don't know why that is. I'm a horrible spender, which is probably why I've gone broke so many times.

Better to just make more with many streams of income so you don't have to worry about going broke. And then saving will come naturally as you make more money. Don't forget that a salary will never make you money. After taxes and the daily grind, and your exhaustion and the feelings of "I hate my job", and then inflation and then new expenses (kids), you will never be able to save. Avoiding Starbucks every day won't make you a millionaire, that's a fact. I say it glibly, "try to make more money". I know it's not that easy. But in the long run, if you have a constant focus on alternative ways to make more money, then you will.

R) What Else Should I Do With My Money?

Forget about it. Money is just a side effect of health.

I talk a lot about the daily practice I started doing when I was at my lowest point. I know now after years of doing it that it has worked. I've done very well with it, and I started doing it when I was dead broke, lonely, angry, depressed, and suicidal. I didn't start it from a position of privilege. Here's the whole thing: stay physically healthy in whatever way you know how (sleep well, eat well, exercise). Be around good people who love you and respect you and who you love and respect, and be grateful every day.

Think of new things each day (or all day) to be grateful for. "Gratitude" is another word for "Abundance" because the things you are most grateful for, become abundant in your life.

And finally, write down 10-20 bad ideas a day. Or good ideas. It doesn't matter. After exercising my idea muscle for six months, I felt like an idea machine. It was like a super power that just wouldn't stop. More on this in another post. Money and abundance in your life is a natural side effect of the above. I know this for myself but now since writing about it for almost four years I can tell you from the letters I get that it works for others.

S) What's In It for You?

I don't know. I used to write about money stuff because I wanted investors, or I wanted to sell books, or get speaking engagements. Now I want none of that. But I get worried that in a world of increasing economic uncertainty that more and more people are getting "stuck" and are scared about what is happening. Too many people I know are nervous and depressed. There's nothing else to know about investing your money. If your bank tries to give you any advice just say, "thanks but I'm ok".If they want you to put your money in a savings account, even "so you can get the interest" I would politely decline. There's a reason they are asking you to do this and I have no idea what it is but it's not good for you. You won't get rich investing your money but you can do very well. And if you combine that with investing in yourself, you will get wealthy. But only if you remember that financial wealth is a side effect of real inner wealth. This is the most powerful investment you can do with your time and your life.

You can always make money back when you've lost it. But one single split moment of stress and anxiety you will NEVER make back again. Investing in the future will never bring back the past. To be able to sit and not have a million stressful thoughts racing through your head. To be able to appreciate everything around you for the abundance it is. Most people think they need to say "thank you" to the world. But the world is constantly saying "thank you" to you for being alive, for creating new things, new energies, new experiences.

Every day give the world at least one more reason to whisper "thank you" to you. If you can hear that whisper, everything else, every gift in life, becomes expected. You earned it.

Just take it.

THE TEN MOST IMPORTANT RULES YOU NEED TO KNOW ABOUT INVESTING

So, now that you have a fly-on-the-wall view of how Wall Street treats people and you know where *not* to invest your money, where *should* you invest your money?

1. *Invest with someone smarter than you.*

   Warren Buffett, for instance, has to file a form every three months called a "13G Form" which lists his holdings. If you study all his 13G forms you can understand roughly what price he bought. Try to buy at a lower price than Buffett did (you may need to wait for a down market). This makes Buffett your free employee. Note, that this means I don't have to worry about all the BS that everyone else thinks about—cash flows , P/E rations, expenses, etc. I assume my buddies at Warren Buffett Inc have taken care of all of that for me. It's important to know one thing – you never really know what's going on inside a public company. Everything is as secretive as possible. So I just trust that Warren Buffett, in some fancy bridge tournament, has figured it all out instead of me using Yahoo Finance. By the way, this applies to everything: commodities, art, bonds, etc. But the key is: the investor I co-invest with HAS to be smarter than me and that can only be demonstrated with an audited track record that ideally has lasted for decades and not just a one-time winner here and there or a guy who is a talking pundit on TV. Only invest with the real winners and often you have to dig to find them but a starting point is the 13G filings at sec.gov. If anything, diversify not across stocks but across the smart people you follow. That is real diversification instead of "Yahoo

Finance diversification."

2. *Remember that cash is king.*

   Having a lot of cash leads to a stress free life. Invest as little as possible.

3. *For wealth creation: Invest in hard-to-value companies that focus on ideas.*

   For example: biotechnology (low revenues/big market)

4. *For wealth-preservation: Invest in dividend aristocrats* (company raising their dividends for twenty years in a row or more) that also follow rule "A."

5. *Allocate.*

   Follow the 3 percent rule: put no more than 3 percent in any one investment. And have 70 percent of your money in cash. When the market crashes, this all changes. A market crash means the market is down 30 percent and at least one newspaper is saying capitalism is dead. At this point, put as much of your money as possible in either high dividend companies that have crashed or private companies where the co-investors are smarter than you. How do you find these co-investors? Go to Angel.co and study all of the private companies that list there and who their private investors are. It's OK if you then experience volatility. In the long run the market will go back to all-time highs like it always does.

6. *For private investing: Invest in at least TWO people smarter than you:* another investor and the CEO of the company who has to have succeeded before.

   Or else, politely turn down the opportunity to flush your money down the toilet.

7. *The S&P 500 index is proven to be the best hedge* against inflation except for hyperinflation.

8. *Investing in you is the best hedge against hyperinflation.* If you have a good business, you collect all the money.

9. *Never invest in anyone else's ideas of investing:* mutual funds, ETFs, bank advisors, hedge funds, venture capital funds.

10. *Never invest because of tax reasons:* 401(k)s, IRAs, Roth IRAs, 529 Plans,

insurance annuities, etc.

These are taxes against the middle class where the money goes straight from your employer into the hands of the rich.

WHAT DO I DO WITH MY OWN MONEY?

I invest myself as I instruct others to. I have *as much in cash as possible.* None in money market funds. Just cash. I own blue chip stocks that pay dividends for wealth preservation and I invest in some hard-to-value idea companies for wealth creation. I'm also invested in about thirty private companies that I primarily invested in the 2009 crash when valuations were extra low and I was always investing with sophisticated investors smarter than me and was always investing in CEOs that had succeeded before.

I spend *money on experiences* and not objects. I don't really own anything except books, some clothes, a phone, a tablet, and a computer. But I'll take my children on extravagant vacations or I'll hold dinners of ten people who don't know each other, or I'll travel to California just to meet someone I want to meet. I don't have a credit card. I don't have debt. This is not because debt is bad. In fact, when interest rates are low it's never a horrible idea to take on some debt. But money is a subset of "things that go *BOOM!*" and I like to be as stress-free as possible.

I choose public over private school. I moved about eighty miles out of NYC so I could send my kids to a good public school and pull them out of the BS private school they are in. I'm in favor of "unschooling"—no school education at all. I trust that kids want to learn and if they don't, then school is even a worse way to get them to learn. School is intended as babysitting so I don't let a BS private school charge college-like prices to babysit my kids.

I lease a car and don't own. "How come?" you might ask. "Cars can last fifteen years now. Why lease?" The reality is a car is just a computer with a car app in it.

Cars will last for fewer years than you think because now the car companies make sure your car breaks down just when the next model comes out. So I lease for three years and then get the next model. Plus, less money down and cash is king.

I rent and I will *never* buy a house again. As discussed previously a house has all the qualities of the worst investment in the world: it takes up too much of your portfolio, it's highly illiquid, and too much leverage, plus it has "negative dividends" (e.g., every year you pay real estate taxes that go up faster than inflation and you pay unpredictable maintenance costs). Unless you are pro at renting and a pro at maintenance and understand all the other hidden costs and fees, you should not own.

When given the choice of investing in someone else's ideas (like a mutual fund or a private company) or my own, *I invest in my own or usually keep assets in cash.* For instance, if you have $10,000, it's silly to put it in the stock market. Keep it in cash. Then if you want to learn photography, buy a good camera and take a photography class, take lots of photos, put them on a blog, blog about the process (in other words, you just invested in you, so you can have an amazing life experience).

I don't spend a lot on insurance. I insure myself against being incapacitated but I have minimal insurance to protect me from paying doctors or dentists. I don't want to pay exorbitant fees for X-rays and MRIs and hospital stays that I can't control, but I can control the number of doctor visits I make, which is zero per year. So why pay the insurance company for those visits? You do have to have insurance for doctor visits for kids, but don't forget: 100,000 deaths per year are reported due to doctor malpractice. But maybe the worst malpractice is to pay the insurance companies to let the doctors do that to you.

I don't hire lawyers. Sometimes you need a lawyer. But for most things you don't. I use legalzoom to set up a company,. To get a divorce, remember the most important thing is that your children will learn from the example you set on how you treat their mother or father. My ex-wife and I wrote up our own divorce agreement and used a lawyer to shepherd it through the court system. Total cost to lawyers: $1,000.

I do hire accountants. I use an accountant to do my taxes. Why do something like that with a program when you know the pros will do a decent job during times when you can be doing other things with your life?

I don't carry much life insurance. I have life insurance *but* I am reducing it as it becomes less necessary and as I get older (where the payments get more expensive).

I give to charity. Give to something that matters to you. I give to Women for Women International. I think that for most charities you have to do severe due diligence to see how they are allocating funds, but I like the way W4W does allocations. I also give to the charities of anyone who has helped me make money in the past. So I regularly give to the leukemia charity of the ex-CEO of a company I invested in, which was sold for a good exit.

I look for ways to give. I'm aiming to have fewer things in my life. I want to die with no possessions. But over the years I have accumulated possessions. So as much as possible I give as gifts things that are important to me but have a lot of value to the people receiving them.

Inheritance. Nobody should inherit more than the minimal they need monthly to get by but still have motivation to go out and make something for themselves. I set up trusts for my kids, not just to guarantee that they'll never have to lie on the floor scared (like I have) but that their kids and their grandkids will hopefully have money to spend.

I value convenience over luxury. I live in a nice enough (rented) house that's right next to the train so I can get into NYC quickly if I have to. It also has the feature that it's about one hundred feet from the local river so it's probably easier for me to take a beautiful walk in nature than just about anyone.

I value convenient travel. I don't try to save. I fly business class whenever I travel. First class is a scam (not much difference between the two other than the prices). I try to stay in AirBnBs instead of hotels, because why pay the same price for a room that I can pay for a five-bedroom brownstone? I use Uber for a car service so I don't have to wait in the cold for a cab. I use Zipcar instead of rental car agencies because Zipcars (or Cars2Go) are everywhere and require zero paperwork. I hate paperwork or waiting on line. (Does anyone like either of those things?).

I'm going to repeat this: *I buy experiences and not things.* I don't like to buy my kids' gifts. But I'll take them places and won't hold back. They will lose and forget the "things" in the long run. But they will never forget the experiences.

And that's about it. I can't think of anything else I do with my money. I don't buy name-brand clothes (many of my pants and shirts I bought in India for about five dollars each). I don't buy any jewelry. I use the wholesale companies that sell to pawnshops to buy things like an engagement ring. Claudia has to remind me to get new shoes when my shoes wear out every two years or so.

Claudia keeps track of all airline and hotel points but I never think about these things. Not that I'm so above them but I have more confidence in my ability to make money than to save money.

Now for *the big mistakes everyone makes.*

Everyone does a very silly math. They say, "If I save a dollar it's the same as if I make a dollar."

This is not true.

If I have $1,000 to my name, then the maximum I can save is $1,000. But the maximum I can *make* is infinite.

I don't spend a lot because I don't have many financial wants. But when I need to spend, I spend. I'm always focused on the infinite.

The common theme is that I don't want stress. I don't want other people holding my money. I want to have good experiences. I don't want to worry.

Please do whatever you can to not worry. That's Rule #1.

What Happened To Me When I Day Traded - Lessons Learned from Day Trading

I was a day trader for many years, and it almost killed me. I made money by making profits on my own money and also taking a percentage of the profits for the people I traded for. I traded up to $40 million or $50 million a day at my peak. I did this from 2001 to 2004. I learned about day trading but I also learned a lot about myself and what I was good at, what I was horrible at, and what I was psychotic at—things that had nothing to do with day trading.

Day trading is the best job in the world on the days you make money. You make a trade, then maybe twenty minutes later you are out of the trade with a profit, and for the rest of the day you think about how much money you made.

However, on a bad day, it's the worst job in the world. I would make a trade, it would go against me, and then I wanted my heart to stop so my blood would stop thumping so loudly.

I did it for years, though, because I was unemployable in every other way. Here's what I learned. All of these lessons I will certainly use today, many years after I stopped day trading.

You can't predict the future. Everyone thinks they can. But they can't. This applies not just to trading but everything. You could be married for ten years and the next thing you know you are divorced and living alone in a sad apartment. You could be healthy all your life and drink your vegetables and exercise and reduce stress, and a year later you could be dead from cancer.

Most of us would have much less stress if we let go of trying to predict the future. You can always seek to increase the odds in your favor. If I don't jump off bridges, for instance, it's more likely I'll be alive a year from now. But certainly a path to unhappiness is thinking the future can be predicted and controlled.

Hope is not a strategy. If you get to the point where you "hope" you don't get ruined, then you did something wrong beforehand. For instance, if you plan a wedding outside and you don't have a backup plan in case it rains, then you probably planned your wedding poorly, unless you are getting married in a desert. "Hoping" in and of itself is not a bad thing. I hope that every day my life goes perfectly. But if hoping is the *only* thing I'm relying on, then it means I didn't really look at all the possible outcomes of something that was important to me.

Uncertainty is your best friend. A hundred percent of opportunities in life are created because people are uncertain about almost everything in their lives. We are constantly trying to close the enormous gap between the things we are certain about and the things we are uncertain about, and almost every invention, product, Internet service, book, whatever has been created to help us close that gap.

Sometimes this is hard. If your husband leaves you, you often feel like crawling on the floor and burning all the self-help books. They all lied. It's hard to feel "in the now" or to "positive think" when life feels like it's over. I've tried. For me it's too hard. But at the very least you can say . . . "help me." You can say it to your close friends. You can say it something inside of yourself. "Help me" is the most powerful, and most forgotten, prayer.

Taking risks involves reducing risk. Some people take too many risks and they go bankrupt. And sometimes people are too cautious and don't take enough risks. When I first started day trading, I was so afraid of risk that I'd end the trade if I had a small profit. But then I would take big losses and that would wipe out all my profits. The key is that you can take larger and larger risks if you work on better ways to deal with those risks. For instance, I might be able to risk marrying someone if I know she is not a hard-core drug addict who regularly betrays the people she is close to. I can risk driving without a license if I always stay below the speed limit (I know this is a stupid risk, but still). Once you have a method of reducing risks, it's easier to make trades or decisions about anything.

Diversification is critical. Often I get e-mails telling me, "I really want *one* job but they don't seem to want me and now I'm miserable. How can I get that job?" Well… you can't. And you're going to be unhappy. You can't wish yourself a job.

When I was raising money to day trade, I probably contacted over 1,000 people. I started over a dozen Internet businesses and watched all of them fail but one. Then when I was trying to sell my Internet business I contacted over a dozen companies (although Google broke my heart—damn you, Google!).

When I wanted to get married, I went on lots of dates. Claudia had an even smarter approach: she wouldn't waste time with dinners. She would only go to tea with guys. Within the first twenty seconds you know if you are attracted. So keep it to a tea.

Say no. If something is not working out in day trading —even if your heart wants it to work out—you have to say no and cut your losses. If a business relationship is not working out, don't put more energy and time into it. There is a cognitive bias called "commitment bias" that leads us to think that just because we've already put time and energy (or money) into something that we have to stick with it. But we don't. Say no to it. You have to decide every moment if *this* is the situation you want to be in. Just because you were in the situation a moment ago, or yesterday, or for ten years, doesn't mean the situation is right for you anymore.

Your health is always important. Day trading pulls everything out of you. It sucks the soul out of your body, blends it up, and then explodes. So you have to take care of yourself. If you don't sleep enough, if you don't eat well, exercise, be around positive people, be grateful for what you have, blah, blah, blah, you will lose all of your money and go bankrupt. And obviously, this applies to everything else in life. So think about it: what small thing can you do every day to become a slightly better you?

The reason we get so attracted to "safe" cubicle jobs is that the pain is subtler and sneaks up on us. It's not the blender drama of day trading, so the need for health on a daily basis doesn't seem as important. But it is.

Laughter is essential. The only way to survive is to laugh. There's that saying:

"Man plans, God laughs." Well, you might as well be on the same side as God, right? Saying "This is crazy" means you're crazy. I've seen it a million times. Guy makes a trade. The market *goes* against him. He says, "This is crazy" and puts more money into the trade. And then he loses all his money and goes crazy. I've had to talk people off the ledge or tell them to put the gun down.

The market is never crazy. The world is never crazy. And I will go so far as to say that your girlfriend who just lied to you about where she spent the night is not crazy. I only care about you. And you're effin' crazy if you thought the world was going to line up any other way than the way it lined up. Tough on you. I know that when I feel like, "ugh, this situation is insane," the first place I need to look is at me. I am insane.

IT DOESN'T MATTER IF A TRADE (OR A DAY, OR A LIFE) IS GOOD OR BAD.

Good and bad days happen. But life is about a billion little moments that add up to all the things around you. If you let one of those moments have too much control, then you are bound to be mostly miserable. I was mostly miserable during the period I was day trading, because I let that aspect of my life take control. I stopped focusing on being a good husband, a good father, a good friend, a good anything. All of my other constituencies went to hell. I would have nightmares. I would lose sleep. I would wake up many mornings and go to the church across the street so I could be by myself and pray. What would I pray? "Jesus, please make the markets go in my direction today."

I'm Jewish. Nobody answered my prayers.

It's never about the money. Every day I get e-mails like, "Can you show me how to day trade?"

"*No!*"

I know a thousand day traders and only two that won't go bankrupt. So what makes anyone think they will have an edge? How many people listen to me? Zero. How come? Because people are sick of their lives, their relationships, their jobs, and all the lies that have been told to them ever since they learned how to walk. They want freedom from the BS.

I get it. Day trading is the dream. You can make enough money to not care. To do it from anywhere. To be happy. It won't work. But people don't want to believe it. Most people think they have that one special something that will make it work for them. And it's true: they do have that one special something. But you can't get there by day trading first.

You can skip right to the being happy part. You can skip right to being free. But we never learned that. We were taught we had to do something first to earn freedom. We were taught that suffering was the currency to buy happiness.

OK, go do it. Then cry about it. Then get scared. Then curse the craziness. Then cry more. None of that will make you happy.

Then read this chapter again. Not because it will make you happy. But because I like when people read my words.

And laugh.

STREET SMARTS ARE VITAL: MENTAL MODELS WORTH LEARNING

I'm not going to recreate the wheel here, since many good writers and thinkers have already developed models for life that have largely worked for them and others. I'm going to describe the ones I think you should learn and where you can read more about them.

I've been really lucky: a lot of the developers of these models have appeared on my podcast and I've been able to ask them more about these models than they revealed in their books. And now you get to reap the benefits of their wisdom. Looks like you're pretty lucky, too.

Antifragile is a book by Nassim Taleb. The word *antifragile* refers to a system that gets stronger as it gets hurt. This is different from being resilient. Resilience is if you get hurt and can stay the same. It's not so bad to be resilient. But it's better to be antifragile.

The book is about whether or not the economic system we live in is antifragile. It's not. It's as fragile as can be which is why I wanted to write this book- to make you personally antifragile regardless of the system.

Before Nassim came on my podcast I told him I wanted to talk about personal antifragility. Specifically, I've never really been sick. So I'm worried that the first time I get sick, I'll just be a whining baby and collapse in pain and agony and die.

We spoke about some of the ways Nassim works on his personal antifragility. For instance, he walks twenty hours ("hours," not "miles") a week. Our ancestors walked constantly for millions of years. "Now," he told me, "we take the car to go two miles to the gym and then we walk on the treadmill for two miles."

We spoke about diets, particularly the paleo diet (i.e., where you essentially eat like a caveman—high fiber, meat, vegetables and fruits, nothing processed/dairy, etc.) that has become popular. He said the big problem with the paleo diet is that it doesn't have random fasting. "Fasting is necessary and has to be random," he said. "Our ancestors never knew where their next meal was coming from. They didn't have breakfast, lunch, and dinner. And almost all ancient cultural practices include some form of fasting."

It's worth reading his book or listening to my podcast interview with him to get more ideas on personal antifragility.

THE FOUR-HOUR WORK WEEK

Tim Ferriss is a good friend who has also come on the podcast. When *The 4-Hour Work Week* came out it was explosive. It turns out that—no surprise—

many people hate work so they want to work less.

But what people think of working four hours and the actual implementation is very different. The basic idea is: build a successful business, figure out what you can outsource or what unprofitable (or barely profitable) clients you can fire, and then use your extra time to explore new ideas.

It doesn't mean just lie on the beach for thirty-six hours.

One thing Tim told me on the podcast that I thought was fun: "I wanted to call the book the "Two Hour Work Week" because that was what was really happening to me. But the publishers didn't think anyone would believe it.

THE 10,000 HOUR RULE

This was popularized in Malcolm Gladwell's book *Outliers*, which I highly recommend just for the section on how the Beatles obtained mastery in playing rock. Basically, they took a gig for a few years where they were playing almost twenty hours a day in German strip clubs. This gave them their 10,000 hours of "practice with *intent*," and that made them the best in the world at rock and roll.

It's not just practice, but practice with intent that's important. (Review the chapter on mastery in part 1 for more details how to do this.)

The 10,000 hour rule is important. Can it be avoided? Can something be mastered in less than 10,000 hours?

Yes, and no.

If you don't need to be in the top 0.001 percent, then yes, you can cut down your hours significantly and still be better in a field than 90 percent or 80 percent of the population, which is enough in most fields to demonstrate mastery (as opposed to being the best in the world.

Many fields of life have very steep learning curves and then very slow learning curves after a certain point. I'd rather spend 2,000 hours each on five areas of life with very steep learning curves, get in the top 10 percent of all of those, rather than spend 10,000 hours on one area of life.

Idea Sex

If you combine two areas of life and get reasonably good at both and then combine them, then you are suddenly the best in the world at the combination. Google is a great example. Larry Page was an academic at heart but he built a search engine. Then he combined it with the idea of how academics rank the value of their papers. Putting the two together gave him the basic algorithm of Google, dubbed PageRank, and Google became the best search engine in the world.

The 80-20 Rule

Tim Ferriss talks about this in his various books, and it's a notion that's been around for a long time. It was originally discovered when someone noticed that 80 percent of the land in Italy was owned by 20 percent of the people. The basic idea is that 20 percent of your effort will result in 80 percent of your results. For instance, 20 percent of your clients will result in 80 percent of your profits. Twenty percent of what you practice in tennis will result in 80 percent of your wins. Twenty percent of your employees will do 80 percent of the work. This rule works in almost every area of your life.

What I like about the 80-20 Rule is that it can be applied to itself. In other words. Take the 20 percent that produces results and apply it again. Now 4 percent (20 percent of the 20 percent) of your work results in 64 percent (80 percent of the 80 percent) of your results. Applied again and 1 percent of your work roughly creates 50 percent of your results.

Understanding this rule and it's applications is what led to that of *The 4-Hour*

Work Week and can also help reduce the 10,000 Hour Rule so that you can learn very efficiently only the things you need to learn to be perceived as a master in a field.

———∞———

THE ONE PERCENT RULE

I forget where I read it. But basically I live my life by this rule. If you try to improve in some area of your life one percent a day, then in one year you will be thirty-eight times better than you were at the beginning of the year. These numbers don't make a lot of sense in much of personal life (for instance, will you be a thirty-eight-fold better husband if you put in one percent more effort every day? Maybe!). But I always try to find at least one thing that I can improve one percent at each day. Then I know that everything is in the direction of small improvement and within a year I will be, in some weird notion, thirty-eight times better.

———∞———

THE FOUR AGREEMENTS

This is the title of a book by Don Miguel Ruiz. It's intended as an inspirational book but I like the four simple agreements he makes with himself to make his life better.

I recommend reading the book but I'll describe the agreements here:

1. **BE IMPECCABLE WITH YOUR WORD.** This is not the same as radical honesty where you just spew everything out of your mouth that is "honest." It just means if you say you will do something, do it. If you feel like you have to lie to make excuses, then just don't say anything at all.

2. **DON'T TAKE ANYTHING PERSONALLY.** This is valuable advice in this era of Internet trolls and "outrage porn."

3. **DON'T MAKE ASSUMPTIONS.** If someone is upset at you, for instance, who knows what might be going on in their life that you have no idea about? Also, don't assume you won't get a raise, or that someone doesn't like you. Be curious. Ask questions. Be simple about finding out the truth in a situation before you jump to any assumptions.

4. **ALWAYS DO YOUR BEST.** If you know you aren't cutting corners and always doing your best, then guaranteed you will do exactly the job you need to do.

I describe many other methods for success throughout this book. But I wanted to include these models because they can be read about elsewhere and they've changed the ways in which I live my life.

Not everything is about being the best in the world. Sometimes it's good to have fun. In the next chapter I describe what I do to make my life personally easier. Perhaps it can help you. Perhaps it can help you come up with your own ideas on how life can be easier.

———— ⌘ ————

FOUR THINGS I DO THAT CAN CHANGE YOUR LIFE IN THE NEXT TEN MINUTES

I'm going to be dead for about 9 or 10 trillion years. and probably only alive for the next forty or so. It sounds like I'm trying to put things in perspective. But I'm not. It's just true and even a little depressing. I've never built a rocketship that will make it into space. I'll never cure cancer. I might not even write a best-selling novel about a teenage girl that falls in love with a dominating billionaire.

What will I do? Someone on the question-and-answer site Quora asked, "What can I learn in ten minutes that will be useful for the rest of my life." *This* I can do. I can show you four insanely stupid things that will make the rest of your life better. Sometimes they work and sometimes they don't.

I have 203,433 unread emails not counting my spam box. Not only will I never launch a rocket into space I will never even read all the emails addressed to me. I don't like the term *life hack*. It takes a lot of work to be really good at something in life. You need: a teacher, a passion, read a lot of books, practice three to four hours a day for many days. There are no shortcuts to learning something.

Even if you have every life hack in the book, this is what it takes to be GREAT at something you love doing. Great enough to make a living or even wealth at iteverything takes time and effort. I've done enough interviews now on my podcast with people who the best in the world at what they do and I can see there are no real shortcuts. This is true no matter what field. So instead, I'm going to tell you four dumb things I do that I have fun with and has made life *a lot* smoother for me. Since there are no real rules to life I would encourage you to seek out the four of five or ten or twenty things that give you fun, and makes life a little easier for you.

1. USE TWO-DOLLAR BILLS

I have thousands of two-dollar bills. I always tip with two-dollars bills. How come? Because then people remember me. They always say, "whoah! I've never had one." And then the next time I come into an establishment, I'm remembered. This is good for restaurants, dates, poker night with friends, even for paying at the local deli. I also find that this is a quick way to make friends whenever I move to a new town. I'm very shy and this gets people talking. This has also been very good on dates. Nobody ever forgets the guy with a roll of two-dollar bills.

2. WEAR A DOCTOR'S COAT

I wear a doctor's lab coat most of the time. Like in airports, restaurants, walking around town. The reason?

- It's comfortable.

- The big pockets let me put any electronic devices I might need—an iPad Mini, for example, plus waiter's pads (see below).

- People *actually* do treat me like a doctor. If someone said, "I need a doctor" I would not be able to help (unless it's easy stuff in which case I can say, "I'm not a doctor" and then perform CPR or mouth-to-mouth or Heimlich, which are all easy to learn.) But the reality is, people move out of the way if you are in an airport and walking around in a doctor's coat. And in restaurants sometimes people let me go first. Is this unfair? Well, I never claim to be an *actual* doctor. I'm just wearing a doctor's coat because I like how it feels, looks, and the functionality of it. But if it has other benefits, which it does, I'll take it. Besides, 99.99 percent of the time someone goes to the doctor here is the correct answer the doctor should give: "Go home and sleep more. Call me in a year."

3. USE WAITER'S PADS

I spoke about this in an earlier chapter, but it's such a benefit for me that I'll say it again. I have about three waiter's pads. I order them for about ten cents a pad in bulk on a restaurant supplies website.

I use them to write at least ten ideas a day. Don't keep track of the ideas. Just become an idea machine.

I use a pad instead of a laptop or iPad because a screen messes with your dopamine levels. I like the visceral experience of putting pen to pad. Specifically, a waiter's pad forces you to be concise. A waiter's pad has a limited number of lines. You can't write a novel there.

And I've said how it's a great conversation piece in meetings. How once I pull out the waiter's pad someone always says, "I'll take fries with my burger" and everyone laughs. Again, I'm shy so it's a good way for me to break the ice. When you pull out a waiter's pad in restaurants, guess what happens? Waiters treat you better.

4.iv. The other day in a cafe I was working and someone potentially violent came up and asked me for money. I held up my waiter's pad and said, "I'm a waiter, do you want to order something?" and they sort of looked at me and grunted and then walked away.

Watch Standup Comedy

I touched on this in the chapter on public speaking, but watch stand-up comedy before every meeting, date, dinner, media appearance, conversation, public talk. I watch Louis CK, Daniel Tosh, Amy Schumer, Anthony Jeselnik, Jim Norton, Andy Samberg, Seth Rogen, Marina Franklin, Ellen, Bo Burnham, and maybe a dozen others.

I have a lot of inhibitions when I meet people. I'm scared and somewhat introverted. Stand-up comedians are the best public speakers in the world and quite frequently, the most astute social commentators on the human condition. So I watch them before most social encounters— personal, professional, media— because it gives me a boost of energy. My "mirror neurons" are going to feed off of their boost of energy for at least one to three hours after I watch them. It gives me material. I won't steal from a comedian (yes I will). And at the very least, I often improvise based on material I heard a comedian said.

I'm not competing with them. I'm just on a date. Or a business meeting. Studying the subtleties of how comedians get laughs: their timing, their voices, their silences, the way they look at the audience, the way they move across the stage, the way they benefits from the comedians who came before them, *and* their actual commentary about life, helps me in my many interactions with people.

Anyway, those are the four insanely stupid things that I wanted to share.

And they work.

How to Get an MBA from Eminem

In 2002 I was driving to a hedge fund manager's house to hopefully raise money from him. I was two hours late. This was pre-GPS and I had no cell phone. I was totally lost.

I kept playing "Lose Yourself" by Eminem over and over again. I was afraid this was my one shot and I was blowing it. I was even crying in my car. I was going broke and I felt this was my one chance. What a loser.

Finally I got there. The hedge fund manager was dressed all in pink. His house was enormous. Maybe 20,000 square feet. His cook served us a great meal. I had made him wait two hours to eat. And he had cancer at the time. I felt real bad. Eventually I did raise money from this manager and it started a new life for me. But that's not why I bring up Eminem at all.

The song "Lose Yourself" is from the movie *8 Mile*. Although I recommend it, you don't have to see it to understand what I am about to write. I'll give you everything you need to know.

Eminem is a genius at sales and competition and he shows it in *one* scene in the movie. A scene I will break down for you line by line so you will know everything there is to know about sales, cognitive bias, and defeating your competition. First, here's all you need to know about the movie. Eminem is a poor, no-collar, white-trash guy living in a trailer park. He's beaten on, works crappy jobs, gets betrayed, etc. But he lives to rap and break out somehow.

In the first scene he is having a "battle" against another rapper and he chokes. He gives up without saying a word. He's known throughout the movie as someone who chokes under pressure and he seems doomed for failure. Until he *chooses himself.* The scene that really drives this point home, for me at least, is the final battle in the movie. He's the only white guy and the entire audience is black. He's up against the reigning champion that the audience loves. And he wins the battle. You can use the techniques Eminem employs to go up against any competition. First off, watch the scene (with lyrics) before and after my explanation. Go to

YouTube and type *"Eminem rap battle vs Papa Doc 8 Mile lyrics."*

Watch it right now.

Done? OK, let's break it down.

How did Eminem win so easily? One very important way we humans evolved is that the brain developed many biases as shortcuts to survival. Setting aside his talent for a moment (assume both sides are equally talented), Eminem used a series of cognitive biases to win the battle.

For instance, we have a bias toward noticing negative news over positive news. The reason is simple: if you were in the jungle and you saw a lion to your right and an apple tree to your left, you would best ignore the apple tree and run as fast as possible away from the lion. This "negativity bias" is the entire reason newspapers still survive today.

We no longer need those shortcuts as much. There aren't that many lions in the street. But the brain took 400,000 years to evolve and it's only in the past fifty years maybe that we are relatively safe from most of the dangers that threatened earlier humans. Our technology and ideas have evolved, but our brains can't evolve fast enough to keep up with them. Consequently, these biases are used in almost every sales campaign, business, marketing campaign, movie, news, relationships—everything.

In-Group Bias

Notice Eminem's first line: "Now everybody from the 313, put your motherf&cking hands up and follow me."

The 313 is the area code for Detroit. And not just Detroit. It's for blue-collar Detroit, where the entire audience, and Eminem, is from. So he wipes away the out-group bias that might be associated with his race and he changes the conversation to "who is in 313 and who is not in 313."

Herd Behavior

Put your hands up and follow me, he says. Everyone starts putting their hands up without thinking. So their brain tells them that they are doing this for rational reasons. For instance, they are now following Eminem.

Availibility Cascade

The brain has a tendency to believe things if they are repeated, regardless of whether or not they are true. This is Availability Cascade. Notice Eminem repeats his first line. After he does that he no longer needs to say "follow me." He says, "Look, look." He is setting up the next cognitive bias.

Distinction Bias or "Out-groups" Bias

Brains have a tendency to view two things as very different if they are evaluated at the same time as opposed to if they are evaluated separately.

Eminem wants the audience to see his opponent "Papa Doc" as someone different from the group, even though the reality is they are all in the same group of friends with similar interests, etc. Eminem says: "Now while he stands tough, notice that this man did not have his hands up." In other words, even though Papa Doc is black, like everyone in the audience, he is no longer "in the group" that Eminem has defined and commanded: the 313 group.

He has completely *changed the conversation* from race to area code.

Ambiguity Bias

He doesn't refer to Papa Doc by name. He says "this man." In other words, there's "the 313 group" that all of us in the audience are a part of, and now there is this ambiguous man who is attempting to invade us.

Watch presidential campaign debates. A candidate will rarely refer to another candidate by name. Instead, he might say, "All of my opponents might think X, but we here know that Y is better." When the brain starts to view a person with ambiguity it gets confused and *can't make choices* involving that ambiguity. So the person without ambiguity wins.

◦✐◦

CREDENTIAL BIAS

Because the brain wants to take shortcuts, it will look for information more from people with credentials or lineage than from people who come out of nowhere.

So, for instance, if one person was from Harvard and told you it was going to rain today and another random person told you it was going to be sunny today you might be more inclined to believe the person from Harvard. Eminem uses this subtly two lines later. He says, "one, two, three, and to the four." This is a direct line from Snoop Dogg's first song with Dr. Dre, "Ain't Nothin But a G Thing." It is the first line in the song and perhaps one of the most well-known rap lines ever. Eminem directly associates himself with well-known successful rappers Dr. Dre and Snoop when he uses that line.

He then uses Availability Cascade again by saying, "one Pac, two Pac, three Pac, four." First, he's using that one, two, three, and to the four again but this time with Pac, which refers to the rapper Tupac. So now he's associated himself, in this little battle in Detroit, with three of the greatest rappers ever.

◦✐◦

IN-GROUP/OUT-GROUP

Eminem points to random people in the audience and says, "You're Pac, he's Pac," including them with him in associating their lineages with these great rappers. But then he points to his opponent, Papa Doc, makes a gesture like his head is being sliced off and says, "You're Pac? *None.*" Meaning that Papa Doc has no lineage, no credibility, unlike Eminem and the audience.

Basic Direct Marketing: List the Objections Up Front

Any direct marketer or salesperson knows the next technique Eminem uses. When you are selling a product, or yourself, or even going on a debate or convincing your kids to clean up their room, the person or group you are selling to is going to have easy objections. They know those objections and you know those objections. If you don't bring them up and they don't bring them, up then they will not buy your product.

If they bring it them before you, then it looks like you were hiding something and you just wasted a little of their time by forcing them to bring it up. So a great sales technique is to address all of the objections in advance. Eminem's next set of lines does this brilliantly.

He says, "I know everything he's got to say against me."

And then he just lists them one by one:

"I am white."

"I am a fucking bum."

"I do live in a trailer with my mom."

"My boy, Future, is an Uncle Tom."

"I do have a dumb friend named Cheddar Bob who shot himself with his own gun."

"I did get jumped by all six of you chumps . . ."

And so on.

By the end of the list, there's no more criticism you can make of him. He's addressed everything and dismissed it. In a rap battle (or a sales pitch), if you address everything your opponent can say, he's left with nothing to say.

When he has nothing to say, the audience, or the sales prospect, your date, your kids, whoever, will buy from you or listen to what you have to say.

Look at direct marketing letters you get in e-mail. They all spend pages and pages addressing your concerns. This is one of the most important techniques in direct marketing.

Humor Bias

Eminem saves his best for last. "But I know something about you," he says while staring at Papa Doc.

He sings it playfully, making it stand out and almost humorous. This is Humor Bias. People remember things that are stated humorously more than they remember serious things.

Extreme Out-group

"You went to Cranbook." And then Eminem turns to his "313 group" for emphasis as he explains what Cranbook is. "That's a private school."

BAM!

There's no way now the audience can be on Papa Doc's side but Eminem makes the outgroup even larger. "His real name's Clarence. And his parents have a real good marriage."

BAM and *BAM!* Two more things that separate Papa Doc out from the crowd. He's a nerdy guy, who goes to a rich school, and his parents are together—unlike those of probably everyone in the audience including Eminem. No wonder Papa Doc doesn't live in the 313, which was originally stated somewhat humorously but is now proven without a doubt.

CREDENTIAL BIAS (AGAIN)

Eminem says, "There ain't no such thing as . . ."and the audience chants with him because they know he is quoting a line from "Halfway Crooks!" the song by Mobb Deep (I did their website back in 1998), another huge East Coast rap group (so now Eminem has established lineage between himself and both the West Coast and the East Coast).

And by using the audience to say "Halfway Crooks" we're all in the same group again while "Clarence" goes back to his home with his parents at the end of the show.

∾

SCARCITY

The music stops, which means Eminem has to stop and let Papa Doc have his turn. But he doesn't. He basically says, "F*ck everybody," "F*ck y'all if you doubt me." "I don't wanna win. I'm outtie."

He makes himself scarce. After establishing total credibility with the audience he basically says he doesn't want what they have to offer.

He reduces the supply of himself by saying he's out of there. Maybe he will never come back. Reduce the supply of yourself while demand is going up and what happens? Basic economics. Value goes up. He's so thoroughly dominated the battle that now, in reversal to the beginning of the movie, Papa Doc chokes. He doesn't quite choke, though. There's nothing left to say. Eminem has said it all for him.

There's no way Papa Doc can raise any "objections" because Eminem has already addressed them all. All he can do is defend himself, which will give him the appearance of being weak. And he's so thoroughly not in the 313 group that there is no way to get back in there. There's simply nothing left to say. So Eminem wins the battle. And what does Eminem do with his victory? He can do anything. But he walks away from the entire subculture. He walks off at the end of the movie with no connection to what he fought for. He's going to choose himself to be successful and not rely on the small-time thinking in battles in Detroit.

He's sold 220 million records worldwide. He discovered and produced 50 Cent, who has sold hundreds of millions more (and is another example of a "choose yourself-er," as Robert Greene so aptly describes in his book *The 50th Law*).

Doesn't it seem silly to analyze a rap song for ideas on how to be better at sales and communicating? I don't know. You tell me.

I've exposed myself so much in my writing. I've been really embarrassed. In fact, I don't "publish" anything unless I'm afraid of how people will react. When you expose yourself there are many ways for people to attack you. People will stab you and hurt you. But you can't create art unless you show how unique you are while being inclusive with others who share your problems.

AVOID REGRETS

Everyone wants to know what dead people say right before they die. Words maybe infused with speckles of a heaven. Beethoven supposedly said on his deathbed, "Friends, applaud! The comedy is finished!" Lou Costello said, "This was the best ice cream soda I ever tasted."

A question similar to this is, "What are common regrets of people in their thirties and forties?" And, can we avoid them if we know what they are?

Well, here are my regrets. And each one can be organized around one word: Don't.

DON'T BUY THINGS

I have said it before, but I'll repeat: buy *experiences*. A house is a thing. An experience is a trip. An experience is a visit to that girl or guy on the other side of the world who said, "Maybe." An experience is an invitation to meaning instead of material. A thing eventually gets thrown away. An experience is a memory you'll have forever.

⸎

Don't Do Anything You Don't Want to Do

You think you have time to get out of it. But you don't. And then it happens. And then it's too late. And then it's something you did. You were the target and you got shot. A black ink stamp leaving its mark on your wrist. You went to the party and the next day, all blurry and inky, it shows and everyone can see. And now all you can think about is what you would have done with that time or how you would have spent that money instead of buying $ fifteen cocktails.

⸎

Don't Try to Please People

Nobody is more worthy of love in the entire universe than you. I wish I had reminded myself of that more. I could've saved all of that time where I was trying to please someone else. Money you lose you can always make back. But even five minutes of time lost is gone forever.

⸎

Don't Fall in Love With Someone Who is In Love With Somebody Else

These people are magnets of love. They've sucked all the love out of the room so when you walk in, it's already too late, you're past that zone in the black hole where nothing ever gets out and nobody ever knows what's there. It's lost in space and time. When I've fallen in love with someone who was in love with someone else, only pieces of me have ever survived. And even then I had to put those pieces back together into the Tinkertoy robot that became me for a long time.

Don't Make Promises You Can't Keep

And to that I can only say, I'm sorry to that one girl.

⁂

Run, Don't Walk

I don't mean run to a goal or a destination. There are no goals and you realize this around the age of thirty or so. I mean just "run." You build up your blood vessels. More oxygen gets to the brain. You get smarter. Life is better. And you'll see more in life than the people who are walking. Who take their time failing. Who take their time falling for others. Who take their time while waiting for the right moment. Waiting for the right weather, the right coordinates, the right person, to drop anchor. There's never a right moment. So just run to get there.

⁂

Don't Wait for Them to Say Yes

Who is "them"? What are they saying yes to? What do you think will happen after the wait is over? Yes. That's my point. All of the answers to these questions are lesser versions of what happens if you don't wait so I'll say it again. "Don't wait for them to say yes." Say yes to yourself first and everyone will say yes later.

⁂

Don't Steal Paper Clips from The Office

It seems small. But a million paper clips in life add up to what you are, a mish-mash of twisted metal. Be honest. Honesty compounds until your word becomes The Word. Try it and see.

⁂

Don't Consume Bad Things

I mean McRibs, but also I mean the news. And dramas that kill lots of people. And coworkers who gossip in the hallway, everyone trying to pull everyone else down. And family who yells at you only because you have become the piano they play their own anguish on. And late nights with the girl who smiles but you know it will never work. At twenty, life can either compound into beauty or into insanity. This is the "don't" that forks into both.

༄

Don't Regret

It may look like these are regrets. But they are just tattoos that live on me right now. Don't time travel into the past, roaming through the nuances as if they can change. Don't bookmark pages you've already read. Today it starts all over again. Every tomorrow is determined by every today.

I've been to every part of the prison. I went to school. I've bought and lost two houses. I've been married, divorced, remarried.

I've started over twenty businesses and failed at seventeen of them. I've also run a hedge fund and a venture capital fund. I've started and run software companies. I've managed thousands of people. And I've been on the floor lonely and scared to death and wishing I could just press a button to end it all. And it was out of that, that I had to find the way to recover, to finally put it behind me. To finally break free.

I can't say I succeeded at it. Freedom is not a point in time where before that point you were enslaved and after that point you are free. Freedom is something that you practice every day.

If you do everything I've discussed in this book you will gradually make more and more money and help more and more people. At least, I've seen it happen for me and for others. I hope this doesn't sound arrogant. But I've messed up too much by not following the advice I've laid out. So I really had no choice but to

261

share it with you.

Don't plagiarize the lives of your parents, your peers, your teachers, your colleagues, and your bosses. Be the criminal of their rules.

Create your own life.

I wish I were you because if you follow my advice, then you will most likely end up doing what you love and getting massively rich while helping many others. I didn't do that when I was twenty. But now, at forty-six, I'm really grateful I have the chance every day to wake up and improve one percent. And I hope you do the same.

How to Run a "Choose Yourself" Meetup

A lot of what you've read in this book will come to life when you discuss it with other people. So I thought carefully about what the ideal components of a "Choose Yourself" meetup would look like. Choosing yourself requires that you make your own networks and connections that can allow you to continue along the themes of your life. Freedom is the result. More calm is the result. Less conflict in your life is the result. A "Choose Yourself" meetup will, over repeated meetings, automatically lend itself to increasing the benefits of doing a daily practice. I encourage anyone to form one and run it.

By the end of the meeting, people will reap several benefits:

- Ideas on how they can change up or improve their daily practice.
- Ideas on how they can move away or get less dependent on the gatekeepers in their life.
- Ideas on networking. We all need help from others to succeed, pay our bills, meet our obligations, and move forward. Having the support or even simply meeting people who have a similar mindset would certainly help.
- Human contact. The life of someone who chooses him- or herself can be lonely at times, the meetings can ensure that we socialize and have fun.

So here's what I think an optimal "Choose Yourself" meetup would look like. And by the way, if you recognize some themes from twelve-step meetings of Al-Anon or AA, you are right. Those meetings have been working fine for over one hundred years. The model works, people attend and they benefit, so why not? By using their models we get hundreds of years of popular consensus on the best ways to get everyone to

- Participate.
- Feel welcome.
- Speak up.
- Mingle.
- Share their own stories without interruptions.
- Respect each other.
- Keep gossip to a minimum.
- Handle the group financials.
- Choose themselves.
- Improve their lives.

Also, each meeting can, through their own "monthly" or "periodically" business meeting, modify their own format. Each meeting can choose itself; its group can do its own thing, provided that the members of the group agree on it.

We suggest a meeting of an hour or an hour and a half to start. At the stipulated time the meeting starts, exactly on time as this is a sign of respect. The moderator speaks:

Hello, my name is X and I today choose myself. I am the chair for this meeting, and that does not mean I own anything or direct anything, I am just member of the community doing service for a specified period of time.

(At this point a notebook might be passed around with dates of future meetings for people to write down their names for when they are available and willing to chair a meeting.)

People attending this meeting are welcome to chair any of our meetings, because when we rotate the leadership, and follow meeting guidelines, we ensure that we put principles before personalities and that we keep the focus on what is important: choosing ourselves for success.

In the spirit of camaraderie and for the highest good of all, we do not criticize, gossip, interrupt or talk over each other. We respect the order of the meeting.

We remember to put principles before personalities, and if someone feels uncomfortable at any time, anyone can ask the chair to read this introduction again.

Any discussions about changes or improvements to our meetings should be brought up in the business meeting, which for this meetup is held every Xth of the month.

We also do not focus on criticizing, or complaining about people who are not here. We do not blame others or put anyone down. Instead we focus on ideas and healthy partnerships that can help each of us move forward toward creating the life we want. We know that choosing ourselves starts with our own health, and we start with that, with getting to a place of health for us, regardless of other people in our lives.

In short, we put the focus on the life we want to create, and not on regrets of the past.

The only purpose of this meeting is to choose ourselves, become idea machines, and help each other surpass gate-keepers that may appear to stand between us and a rewarding and successful life, for today.

Explain that the format of the meeting consists of reading for fifteen minutes from either *Choose Yourself!*, *The Choose Yourself Guide to Wealth,* or *The Choose Yourself Stories.* Follow this with an introduction of every member and then break the meeting into separate sections to address issues that will help members choose themselves for success.

We remind everyone that whatever is said in this meeting is confidential and must not leave the room. Confidentiality allows all of us to feel safe and share our deepest vulnerabilities. Keeping these meetings confidential is a sign that we are willing to be altruistic, and ready to create a safe space for everyone to choose themselves.

Now let's go around the room and introduce ourselves by first name only and share one sentence on something you did during this week to bring the Daily Practice alive.

E.g.: *"Hi, I'm Mary and this week I've been making lists with ten ideas per day"* or *"I slept eight hours a day, I spent time with my friends,"* or *"I'm very grateful each day for ten things."*

If you are a newcomer we welcome you and hope that the meetings can help you as much as they are helping us.

(Go around the room.)

TIMEKEEPER

We need a timekeeper who will be willing to time the fifteen minutes of the reading and later on the three-minute shares. Participation is key to success; if you usually hide by blending with the background we encourage you to try and do service like that of keeping time for others. Do we have a timekeeper?

Thank you, X, for your service.

Everyone please keep an eye on the timekeeper and respect his or her signals. When the timekeeper says that the time is up please acknowledge his or her and say I will wrap up, and finish, so we can all share.

FIFTEEN-MINUTE READING

Now lets read from [*Choose Yourself!*/*The Choose Yourself Guide to Wealth*].

The book will be passed around and each of us will read two paragraphs. If you do not want to or cannot read, simply pass the book to the next person.

Although we highly encourage your participation, we understand if you simply can't do it for any reason.

OPTION #2

Some groups may opt to change the reading of the book if there is a person who can share their story of how they choose themselves, in that case, the person will speak for fifteen minutes. There will be no interruptions, no questions and no cross talk. The qualification for a "speaker" or "qualifier" is that she or he has been to at least twelve meetings and has been a member of the *"Choose Yourself"* meetings for six months, and, has a "Choose Yourself" story to tell.

OPTION #3

Once a month, or once every so often, the meetings need to have a *business meeting* because it is key to maintaining the finances/electing new chairs (for example if the meetings happen monthly and we need a quarterly person to commit to running the scripted meetings) / select a "library person" who will use funds from the treasurer to buy a book if it is needed, select a "treasurer" etc. The meeting is timed at ten minutes. And it runs like this:

1. **OPEN:** Read minutes from the last business meetings. Treasurer's report he or she says how much money there is in reserve, if we are on time paying the rent and the meetup fees, etc.

2. **LIBRARY REPORT:** do we need to have a book for new comers? Can we get money from the treasurer to do so?

3. **OLD BUSINESS FOLLOWED BY NEW BUSINESS:** People propose ideas, if one is proposed it needs to be seconded, and then there is discussion and voting. If time is running out things can be tabled for the next meeting

DONATIONS

Now, before we move on to shares we will pass a basket around for donations. We do have some fees associated with the meetup and the rental of a room, and a suggested donation is three dollars [never more than five], but if you cannot do it, we understand, please keep coming back because we need you more than your money.

SHARING:

Until fifteen minutes before the closing of the meeting

The floor is now open for sharing. Please remember to acknowledge the time-keeper, do not talk about other people in the room and keep your sharing to your own experiences. Cross talk or criticizing is not accepted as we keep the focus on ourselves. We share our stories of how we are choosing ourselves and the experiences we encounter along the way.

Fifteen minutes before the meeting ends: Gatekeepers, permission networking, and idea sex.

FIVE MINUTES: GATEKEEPERS

We are now fifteen minutes from the end of the meeting so we will discuss gatekeepers.

By show of hands people ask permission to speak and the facilitator picks the first person, who in turn, when finished, will pick the next.

If nobody volunteers, then the facilitator can do the first share, or wait until someone wants to share.

If you are experiencing a "gatekeeping" situation you can share it with us and we will listen. There will be no cross talk, but in the after-meeting if anyone cares to share or help one another you can do so.

Volunteers can describe the gatekeepers that are in their way. For instance, they just submitted a book to a publisher. Or they are hoping for a promotion from their boss. There will be no cross talk, and networking is highly encouraged after the meeting.

People will have suggestions but it's hard to follow suggestions. Everyone has to come up with the solutions from inside. By sharing in the open we give each other a chance to form new ideas from within.

If nobody is sharing on this you can continue with the next segment.

Five minutes: Permission Networking

Perhaps someone has an idea they want to share with someone at a certain company, or they need a contact. Or maybe someone wants to meet someone from another industry. Or maybe someone wants to meet Richard Branson (space's the limit here). We all have ideas. Some have ideas for themselves, some have ideas for others.

People can simply state: I would like a contact at SalesForce, in the marketing department. Again, no cross talking, if someone is willing to talk to this person the end of the meeting is where these conversations will happen.

If nobody is sharing on this you can continue with the next segment.

Five Minutes: Idea Sex

Probably when people were sharing their Daily Practice of the week, they shared one or two of their ideas (or more) from their idea-list that week. Imagine taking one of your ideas and combining it with one of their ideas, what would result. Some riffing could occur here but no criticism. Every bad idea is an idea and worth exploring.

Ideas are like mazes. You never really know where you are going until you hit the exit. Even a dead end is an opportunity to turn around and explore more of the maze.

Write down ten ideas that you got just by being on the meeting.

Close

We have now come to the close of the meeting, we are grateful that you are here and we hope you benefit from this gathering.

The After-Meeting

There should be at least fifteen to thirty minutes of "after-meeting" where people walk around and talk to one another.

This also gives people a chance to get to know and support one another and to fulfill the second part of the daily practice, which is meeting more and more people who are interested in helping you and supporting you.

About the Author

J ames Altucher's books include the *WSJ* bests-sellers *Choose Yourself!* and *The Power of No*. He is an entrepreneur, chess master, and hedge fund manager. He has started and run more than twenty companies, some of which failed, several of which he sold for large exits.

His writing appears in major media outlets, including the *Wall Street Journal*, the *New York Observer*, Tech Crunch, *The Financial Times*, and others. His blog has attracted more than 20 million readers since its launch.

He hosts three podcasts that have been downloaded over 10 million times. James is the author of fourteen books. Join him at JamesAltucher.com, or Twitter @Jaltucher.

OTHER BOOKS BY JAMES ALTUCHER

Choose Yourself!

The Choose Yourself Stories

The Power of No

50 Alternatives to College

FAQ ME

I Was Blind But Now I See

The Forever Portfolio

Trade Like a Hedge Fund

Trade Like Warren Buffett

CONNECT WITH JAMES

Y ou can ask James a direct question by going to AskAltucher.com and he will answer on his daily podcast. You can also listen to The James Altucher Show, where he interviews people who have chosen themselves for wealth and happiness.

James holds a weekly Twitter Q&A on Thursdays at 3:30 p.m. EST. Join him @Jaltucher.

You can text questions to James's personal cell at 203 512 2161. Don't call him because he never picks up nor has a voicemail. He answers text message questions on Ask Altucher.

And make sure to subscribe to his newsletter to continue the conversation on thinking outside of conventional ways. Do that at JamesAltucher.com.

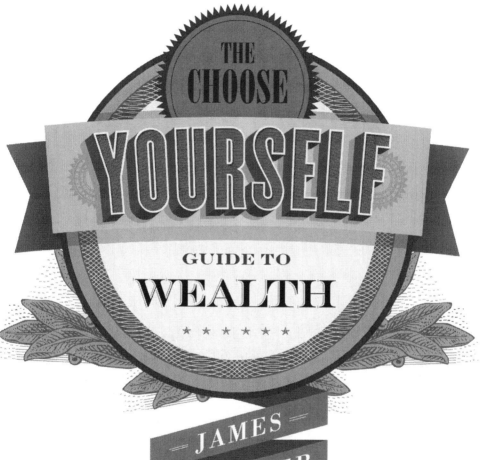